Fashion Knitwits

Fashion Knitwits

ENEIDA MARTINO

ISBN: 1505999391
ISBN 13: 9781505999396

Table of Contents

One

PANTONE, 1984

Fashion Avenue, The City of Fashion, New York City: everything that glitters is not always gold.

I was attending night classes four days a week at Fashion Institute of Technology (FIT) while working during the day in a pharmacy. My major was pattern making and design.

During my break I would sit in a small area near the cafeteria that had a few couches and a coffee table. There was a huge bulletin board nearby filled with fashion ideas, styles, and job listings as well as signs from people selling stuff and looking for roommates. One day I saw an ad on the board that read:

> Receptionist wanted. No experience necessary.
> Monday–Friday, 9–5
> Duties: answering phones, filing, and computer
> Call Human Resources: 212-555-1212

I took the information down and waited until the morning to call. After several attempts I finally got through and spoke to a woman in Human Resources. I scheduled an interview for Monday at 12:30 p.m.

The office was located at 1411 Broadway between Thirty-Ninth and Fortieth Streets, on the tenth floor. She told me that once I got out of the train station, I would see a huge building that circled Broadway and then went around to Fortieth Street, to Seventh Avenue and then to Thirty-Ninth Street and back again to Broadway.

It was only Thursday, but I already knew exactly what I was going to wear: my red interview suit. I'd made it the previous year; it was a double-breasted jacket with black diamond-shaped buttons and a pencil skirt. That suit had gotten me every job for which I'd interviewed.

At eighteen years old, I thought I knew everything about fashion, but really I didn't know anything. I'd grown up in Brooklyn with a single mom and I was the youngest of my three sisters. My mom worked full time. Growing up I would always watch her on the sewing machine, and I wanted to make my own clothes too.

She bought me a sewing machine, and I never looked back. I went to a vocational high school, and my major was fashion. In class we draped muslin on mannequins and made our own patterns. I couldn't sketch, but I was good at sewing a garment together and making a pattern. I won a scholarship to FIT.

I have always dreamed of being a fashion designer.

The Interview

As soon as I walked out of the train station, I saw the building the woman from Human Resources had described to me. It was huge and took up the entire block. As soon as I walked into the building, I saw three humongous chandeliers, a half-moon desk with three security guards sitting behind it, and several elevator banks. On my way up to the office, all I hoped was that I would get the job. I was getting tired of working in that damn pharmacy.

The Pantone offices were on two floors: the tenth and eleventh. I got off on the tenth. There were two glass doors that led into the receptionist's area.

Jovita Ellis was the receptionist on the tenth floor. She was a beautiful woman with red hair and blue eyes. She had been with Pantone for more than fifteen years.

I smiled as I approached the desk. "Hi, my name is Anita Martini, and I have an appointment with Human Resources."

"Have a seat. Someone will be right with you," Jovita said. She had a great smile.

"Thank you," I said.

A woman with curly hair and the ugliest squash-colored suit with matching accessories walked over to me.

"Anita?"

"Yes, hi," I said. We shook hands.

"I'm Sarah. Please follow me."

I filled out an application. Sarah looked it over very quickly.

"Thank you; we'll keep in touch," she said.

That was kind of fast. I stood up quickly. "Oh, OK. Thank you." I walked out of there a bit confused. Maybe it was time to retire the suit.

I stayed home from school and work that Friday because I was not feeling too well. It was more like I was depressed—until my phone rang. I wasn't going to answer it, but then I decided to. It was Sarah Parker from Pantone offering me the job. She asked me when I could start. I started dancing in my pajamas and fluffy slippers. I told her I could start in two weeks. She confirmed the date, and it was official. I took the red suit out of a pile of clothes I was going to donate, kissed it, and then placed it back in my closet.

I immediately called my mom and my sisters and told them the good news. They were so happy for me because they knew I wanted to work for a fashion company. I gave the pharmacy my two weeks' notice.

I spent hours pulling out clothes to wear on my first day. I was so excited I barely slept.

My first day at my new job was filled with meeting people and trying to remember their names. Katie Burke was my supervisor. She was the assistant to the president of Pantone, Dan Bird.

Dan Bird had been the president of the company for more than twenty years. He was six feet tall, with a head of white hair and the bluest eyes. Dan was very nice, but I hardly ever saw him. He was always busy golfing or traveling on business.

Katie had been born and raised in England. She'd been in the States for a few years. I loved her accent. She was about five ten, with pale skin and freckles; short, black hair; and green eyes. Katie and I hit it off. She showed me the ropes and told me about the mailroom and deliveries. Katie told me to page her immediately if her boyfriend, Paul, who still lived in London, called. She introduced me to everyone on both floors and then took me down to Jovita.

"OK, Anita, I'll be back for you before lunch. Jovita will be teaching you the switchboard because you will be relieving her for lunch."

"OK," I said. At that point I would have cleaned the floor just to get to work there. Well...I don't know about that.

The switchboard had about a hundred buttons. Jovita saw the look on my face and said, "It's easy, Anita. You'll get it."

"I hope so."

"Everyone's extension is on the list."

"Cool."

"Oh, *e la estupida*, Katie Burke—watch out for her."

"I didn't know you spoke Spanish."

"Yes, and I grew up in Spain."

"Why did you come New York City?"

"I was a singer in Europe, but I fell in love and moved to Manhattan—to the city that never sleeps."

"Wow, that's awesome. I wish I could sing. Anyway, Katie seems nice."

"Exactly. She seems nice, but she's a bitch. She came close to getting smacked right dead on her face."

"Why? What happened?"

"She thought she could speak to me like a child, and I stopped her dead in her tracks. Not me."

Pantone sold to all the major stores: Le Bon Marché, Bloomingdale's, Saks Fifth Avenue, and Barneys, to name just a few. There was so much to learn, and I was so excited. My responsibilities were to answer the phones, file, and type letters. At first I was a bit shy and nervous about answering the phones, but after a couple of days I became a pro. I knew who was calling who and who was avoiding who. It took me a week to learn the switchboard and most of the extensions.

Pantone offered dental, medical, two weeks of vacation, and unlimited sick days. It sounded great. But what did I know? That would be the best it would ever get. I kept quiet and took what they gave me. I was just happy to have a real job with benefits. The best part of it all was the location: right in the center of the Garment District. There were blocks of stores where I could get all kinds of fabrics, trims, buttons, leather, and anything I needed to make a garment. Everyone seemed so nice. I could have worked there forever.

Being the receptionist and a size eight was perfect because all the samples were size eight, and I could take all the samples I wanted. Every season I had a new wardrobe. I was becoming more fashionable by the day. I loved my job.

I was sitting at my desk one day, daydreaming about how great my job was and thinking that I could get used to working there. Then the phone rang, and I jumped back to the real world. "Good morning. Pantone. Anita speaking."

"Anita, this is Katie. You need to pick up the phone right away. Don't let it go into the third ring. Oh, and your lunch hour is from twelve to one."

"OK."

We hung up. Fifteen minutes later the phone rang again. I picked it up after the first ring.

"Good morning. Pantone."

"Good, I like that. Thank you. Tallyho."

After Katie hung up, I gave the phone the bird. "Bitch."

I called Jovita. She said, "Hey, Anita, what's up?"

"You were right. Katie's a bitch."

Jovita laughed. "I told you."

"I know."

Katie was actually testing me. I really didn't care for people watching me—just let me do my job. Her job was to assist the president, run reports, make reservations, travel arrangements, and take care of other administrative duties. She was training me to create reports for Dan and to put me in charge of her reports. What was I going to say? No? I knew it was her job, but maybe she was overwhelmed and needed help. I was happy to learn; my mother always told me to learn everything I could because I could take that experience with me, and no one could take that away from me.

One day I overheard Dan telling Katie that he needed the reports done by the next week for a big sales meeting. She assured him they would be done. While I was running Katie's reports and answering the phones, she was on the phone talking to her boyfriend in London. I was hoping I didn't mess up because the reports were for the big sales meeting, and Dan was expecting them to be correct. He was expecting Katie to do them right. She would pile paper after paper on my desk and order me to file them because, she claimed, she was working on another project for Dan. Meanwhile she was running up the company's telephone bill.

The next week rolled around, and sure enough, Katie got credit for the reports. As I walked into her office to give her some mail, I heard Dan's voice on her speakerphone.

"Katie," he said.

"Yes, Dan."

"Good job on the reports!"

"Thank you."

I walked away. Katie followed me back to my desk. "Anita, thanks a bunch for the reports."

"Yeah, sure," I said, trying not to show her any attitude.

"Very well. I'm off to my desk." As Katie walked away, she pulled her panties out of her ass. I watched her in disgust. She claimed to be so proper, but she was a nasty pig and probably didn't bathe every day.

I met all the salesmen, and they all seemed very nice. On Monday morning there was a huge breakfast meeting. Dan walked over to me with a big smile.

"Good morning, Anita," he said.

"Good morning, Dan," I said.

"There's a huge spread of breakfast treats in the conference room. Please help yourself."

I smiled at him. "Thank you. I will."

I walked into the conference room and got coffee and a bagel. As I was turning around to walk out, Fred stopped me.

Fred had red hair and millions of freckles. He had lived in Dallas, Texas, and had the accent to prove it.

"So, how's the cunt treating you?" he asked.

I looked at him like he had two heads. "What?"

He laughed. "Katie cuntie is what I call her."

"Oh, she's OK. Why?"

Fred looked around before answering. "She's a bitch. She's always late with my commission checks, and she does it on purpose. I've been waiting for my commission check, and she had it all along." He looked around again and then said, "If she starts with you, call me, and I'll take care of her."

I smiled. "OK, thanks. I have to go back to the front and answer the phones."

As soon as Fred went back into the conference room, Katie came walking toward me really fast and then leaned over the desk. She looked around before speaking. I said to myself, *What's going on here?*

"What was that little ginger asshole telling you?" Katie asked.

"Nothing. Why?"

"Was he talking about me?"

"No," I said.

"Oh, OK. Be careful with him. He likes to lie."

"Yeah, OK. Thanks."

Katie started her usual shit: cleaning papers off her desk and adding them to mine. When she made her final trip, she said, "Oh, Anita, we have more work to do. We have reports due at the end of the month. I'm going to need your help."

I looked dead into her eyes. "Sure." I never said no.

Katie walked away, and the reports became my job. It continued that way for months. I ran reports and did the research while she talked on the phone with her boyfriend.

I answered the phone with an attitude. "Good afternoon. Pantone."

"What's wrong?"

I laughed. "Nothing. Fred?"

"How did you know?"

"Hmm, let me see...The, uh, accent?"

We laughed. "Katie, huh?"

"Yeah, she's dumping all of her work on my desk again. She's a nitwit."

"I'm going to call her."

"No, don't call her!"

"Come on, I'm not that stupid. When her phone rings in a few minutes, I want you to walk over to her desk."

"OK," I said with a smile.

I took Katie one of the finished reports. As I walked into her office, she immediately covered the phone with one hand.

"Yes?" she asked.

"Here is the first report," I said.

"OK. When I'm done, I'll come over to your desk."

That was when her other extension rang.

"Good morning, this is Katie Burke," she said and then paused. "Pardon?" Her face turned beet red. She quickly hung up the phone and then stood up really fast.

"What's wrong, Katie?"

She shook her head. "I have to go to the loo," she said and then ran out of her office.

I went back to my desk and called Fred. "What did you tell her?"

He was laughing so hard, he couldn't answer. After he stopped he said, "I asked to speak to Katie cuntie but in a British accent."

"That was a good one. She ran to the loo."

We laughed again.

"Thanks," I said.

"No problem, kid. My job here is done until the next time. Call me when she starts acting like a cunt, OK?"

—⁂—

After working at Pantone for several months, I was finally comfortable. Twelve o'clock came, and I was out the door for lunch. Katie was starting a bad habit of relieving me ten minutes late. Of course I had to wait for her, and then she had the nerve to ask me if I could pick up some lunch for her. At first I really didn't care, but then it became annoying, and I really didn't know how to tell her. When I got back to the office, she looked pissed. I handed over her lunch, and she snatched it from my hand.

"What's wrong with you?" I asked.

"You're late," she said.

"I'm late? No, I'm not."

"You left at twelve o'clock, and now it's one fifteen."

"Excuse me, but you walked over to me at twelve fifteen, and then I had to go and get your lunch, which took time."

"Can't you do it all within your lunch break?" Katie asked.

"Can't you get your own lunch?"

"Very well. I will."

"Tallyho," I said.

9

She gave me a dirty look, and I smirked at her. That was the end of that. Two hours later she came to my desk with her pile of papers. I was sure she did it on purpose.

"Please file these and create the same report as the last time," she said.

"Sure," I said. I was pissed because I had other things to do. I really liked it at Pantone except for Katie.

She didn't come in for two days, and it was wonderful.

Dan walked over to my desk. "Hi, Anita, how are you?"

"Good, and you?"

"Do you know if Katie started running some reports?"

"Yes, I have them here. I'm working on them," I said.

"Oh, great. Thanks." He walked away and then came back. "Oh, Anita, I forgot to give these to you. These are your clothing-allowance vouchers."

"What do you mean, clothing-allowance vouchers?" I asked.

"With these you can get any clothes you like."

"Really?"

"Yes, really," Dan said as he smiled again.

"These are for me? I can't believe it. Thank you so much."

"Why are you not ripping that envelope open?"

I blushed and smiled. "Oh, of course." I opened it up. The vouchers were for $5,000 each season plus any samples I wanted. "Wow, that's a lot of money. Thank you. Thanks a million."

"Not a problem. Enjoy it, kid."

When Katie came back in, the reports were done, and I was hoping I had done them correctly. They were already on her desk when she walked in.

"Good morning, Katie. How are you feeling?" I asked.

"OK, but not a hundred percent."

I walked with her to her desk. "I put the reports right there," I said.

Katie immediately turned around and in a mean tone yelled, "Where? Where are they, Anita?"

Dan walked in. "Good morning, ladies. Katie, why are you yelling at Anita?"

I smiled and I said, "Katie, I put the reports right there on your desk."

"Good job, Anita." Dan gave me a thumbs-up.

Katie didn't like that at all. She gave me a look that could have killed me, and I stared right back at her. *Bring it.*

After Dan left she turned to me and said, "What are you doing? What are you doing?" She pointed her finger close to my face. "Don't you ever dare do anything behind my back. You're lucky they were correct."

I got really close to her face and pointed my finger back at her, with my teeth clenched. "Don't you ever put your finger in my face. Ever!"

"Pardon?"

"You heard me. You were sick for two days, and I completed the reports. There, done. So what's your problem? I helped you out."

Katie turned and then sat at her desk. She said something under her breath, but I couldn't hear it.

"Pardon?" I asked.

"Thank you," Katie said.

She was nothing but a nitwit, and I would kill her with kindness. I knew that would not be the last time she would ask me to help her. I was sure she would take advantage of me, but at the time I was the one taking advantage of her and learning everything I could.

As I walked back to my desk I heard a sound.

"Pssst. Pssst."

I turned and saw Fred waving me into the kitchen.

"I heard the whole conversation," he said.

"You did? Come, let's walk over to my desk," I said.

"Who the hell does she thinks she is? I'm happy you said something."

"Did you hear Dan yell at her?"

"Yes, I did, but the best part was when you told her off. I loved it."

I nodded. "Yep."

"I'll take care of her." Fred quickly turned around to make sure no one was around. He leaned in close to me. "Can you believe she's always claiming she can't find my commission check?"

"Shh. You're yelling."

He quieted down. "She'd just better find my check because I'll turn her office upside down if she doesn't."

"Did you speak to Dan about it?" I asked.

"No, I haven't had the time to sit down with him. I don't want to sound petty. Plus he thinks she's the best. I'll get it today, or Dan will know about her calls to London."

"You know?" I asked.

"Yep, and so will Dan if she doesn't cough up my fucking check."

"I have to see that. Make sure I'm here before you start."

"How about now?" Fred asked.

Katie went walking by with several envelopes. Fred stepped right in front of her and stopped her in her tracks. My eyes opened wide.

"Did you find my check?" Fred asked.

"No! I haven't," Katie said.

"Well, you'd better because if you don't I'm telling Dan about all those calls to London."

Katie turned as pale as a ghost. "It must be somewhere in my office. When I get back, I will find it."

"I'll wait here," Fred said.

Katie walked away really fast and returned to her office.

Fred turned to me and said, "That's the way she needs to be handled."

I smiled and gave him a thumbs-up. He followed Katie and watched her do something in her office and then he ran back to my desk.

Katie walked over to us. She handed Fred the check. "Here you go."

Fred tried to snatch it from her hand, but she held the envelope with a firm grip. Then she let go. She smiled. As she walked away, Katie said, "Anita I'm going to the post office."

"OK," I said.

"She's evil," Fred said.

There was a piece missing from the top of the envelope. It looked like it had been taped to something and then ripped off. Fred examined the envelope and then looked outside to make sure Katie was gone. He grabbed my arm and said, "Come on."

"Where are we going?" I asked.

We walked to Katie's office. Once inside, Fred pulled me down underneath her desk.

"What are you doing?" I asked. "Aren't you gay?"

Fred laughed. "Yes, stupid bitch, I am. Look!" He pointed under the desk.

"Huh? Oh my God."

"I told you she's always holding my checks hostage!"

Fred matched the ripped section of his envelope with the piece that was taped underneath Katie's desk.

"Oh shit," I said.

As we looked at each other in shock, we heard Katie's shoes hit the wood-panel floors.

"It's her," I said.

"How do you know?" Fred asked.

"Because every morning I study the sound of her shoes, so I know when she's coming."

We tried to stay as quiet as possible and not laugh. Katie walked into her office and moved the chair.

"Oh, there you go," she said and then walked away. She left the office. We ran out of there.

"Oh my God, she had all your checks under her desk," I said.

"I told you she had them. One day when I confronted her about them she told me, 'Look around if you like because I don't have them.' Yeah, under her fucking desk. She's going down."

Things were going great. A few months later Dan retired; Fred resigned; and Katie's visa expired and was not being renewed, so she was forced to go back to London. She was not happy at all. Karma's a bitch.

That was my clue to start looking for another job because things were going to change.

I decided I could find another job the way I had found the one at Pantone. And since I now had some fashion experience, I could find a better-paying job. I have to take out my interview suit. Before Dan left he refered me to his broker, he was looking for an assistant in his brokage firm. I told him ok, but I didn't want to go I wanted to stay in fashion. So I called my sister Lorie to go to the interview for me. She went on the interview and got the job. Everyone was happy.

Jovita and I exchanged numbers so we could keep in touch. I began my search in *Women's Wear Daily*. After a couple of months, I found another job paying more money, and I gave my two weeks' notice.

Two

Sommeil Avec Moi

After Pantone I worked for several small design houses. *Sommeil Avec Moi* means "sleep with me" in French. They manufactured trashy lingerie and accessories. The showroom was on Broadway between Thirty-Seventh and Thirty-Eighth Streets. I was hired as the receptionist. It was a small office.

Carol Mannit was the vice president of sales. She had been with the company for ten years. She was short, blond, chubby, and very pushy.

The designers; accounting; the sample room; and Marlene Kibble, the president of the company, were located on Thirty-Second Street.

Marlene Kibble owned half of the company. Her partner ran another office in France. They had been in business for fifteen years.

Every day Marlene would call the showroom to ask me who was calling for Carol. At first I was honest, but then I wasn't telling her about all the calls. I felt kind of sorry for Carol. I shouldn't have because she was such a catty bitch. I think she had mental problems.

I was not comfortable with everything that was happening. There was so much bickering going back and forth between Carol and Marlene. You would have thought they were still in high school.

Every day I would get stupid remarks over the phone about the name of the company. It got ridiculously annoying, and I started to hate being there. And to top it off, my boss was a bitch with a title. I knew my time there was limited. I needed to get out as soon as I could. I started looking for another job.

One day the phone rang, and it was the perfect time to let Marlene know how I felt.

"Good morning, Marlene," I said.

"Good morning, Anita. Did anyone call for Carol?"

"Oh yeah. About that. I think you should be asking Carol that question. I feel really uncomfortable, and I don't want to get in trouble."

"Don't worry. She will never know it's you unless you tell her."

I was quiet for a few seconds. "I would never tell her."

"So we're clear, right?"

"Crystal."

"Chat with you later. Bye bye."

That was bullshit. Whatever was going on between them, I didn't want to know. I had my own problems. I don't want to get in the middle. It's time to take out my red suit.

Carol would drink and smoke in her office all day. In the '80s people could smoke anywhere they liked. She was such a miserable bitch, especially during market week. When her Saks buyer arrived at the office, I tried calling Carol but there was no answer. I called her again, and there was still no answer. When I walked into her office, I couldn't believe my eyes: she was snoring, with her mouth wide open and a lit cigarette in her hand. What a nitwit.

I walked back to the front and sat the buyer in the showroom. I got her some coffee and a muffin.

"Carol will be with you in a few minutes," I said.

When I went back to Carol's office, she was still snoring, her mouth was still open, and her cigarette was almost burning her fingers.

"Carol! Carol!"

"Mom, I'm up. I'm up," she said.

I was about to burst out laughing, but I pressed my lips together to hold it in. "Saks is here."

"OK, Anita! I will be there in a minute. Where is she?"

"She's in the showroom."

"OK! OK!"

Carol had multiple personalities, and they came to life right in front of me. There were times while in midconversation, she would talk gibberish and then start crying, and then she would laugh. She was a total lunatic. The buyers started complaining to Marlene that Carol was crazy, and they didn't want to work with her.

Carol was all bitchy in her office, but as soon as she walked out to greet the buyer, she was friendly. Several months later I found another job, and I gave my two weeks' notice and moved on.

Three

CHIFFON

Chiffon made blouses and two-piece dressings out of chiffon, silk, satin, and so forth. Their business was very strong and active. The company made a killing selling Chanel lookalike blouses with pleated fronts and black roses on the shoulder blades at cheaper prices.

An Asian woman owned Chiffon. She worked like an animal and expected everyone to work just as hard.

The offices were at 1411 Broadway, on the thirty-fourth floor. The last time I had worked in that building was for Pantone. I liked working there because the subway station was on the same block.

Chiffon hired me as a receptionist. The office was so cramped, it felt like everyone was on top of each other. God forbid someone farted; it would be deadly. Thankfully, as the receptionist I didn't have to deal with the overcrowding.

I always went out for lunch because of the horrible smell of food in the office. It smelled like rotten eggs. Almost all the employees in the back ate at their desks. Imagine the combinations of different foods. They were deadly.

Cindy Kahn was the national sales manager for New York and my boss. She was not all there. She was moody—a nutcase and another bitch with a title. I could see the wickedness in her cold blue eyes. I noticed it right away, and I tried to stay clear of her, but it was hard because the office was so small, and she was my boss.

Several months after I started, my grandfather passed away. I walked into Cindy's office and asked, "You got a minute?"

"Sure."

"My grandfather passed away today."

She smirked like I was bothering her. "Oh my, sorry to hear that."

"I'll be out of the office on Thursday and Friday."

She looked at me. "Really?"

"Yes, really."

"OK, if you say so."

I was talking to a psycho. I didn't think she believed me.

On Monday, when I returned to work, I walked into Cindy's office. "Good morning, Cindy," I said.

With her fake smile, she said, "Good morning, Anita."

I handed her a memorial card with my grandfather's name on it.

"What's this for?" she asked.

"It's for you. It's a memorial card honoring my grandfather."

"Why?"

"It's confirming there was a death in my family. I felt you didn't believe me."

She got all dramatic on me and turned beet red. "Oh my, I would never."

"Well you did!" I walked out of her office. She left it alone because she knew she was wrong. How dare she think I would lie about a family member dying?

Cindy's husband called for her, but she was not at her desk, so I decided to page her: "Cindy, please call the front desk."

She paged me back. "Take a message!" she said with an attitude.

So I paged her back. "OK!" I said it with an attitude too.

From that point on, she was not nice to me. She would look at me with an attitude, and I would do the same to her. I would be damned if I was going to let anyone treat me like shit. She was a nitwit. Just because she was my boss, that didn't give her the right to be mean to me.

The Sample Sale

Twice a year we would have a sample sale to get rid of all the extra units. There was a crew of four women. One would try to distract us by causing a commotion while the other three were busy stuffing merchandise into their stockings underneath their long skirts.

Cindy was such a bitch with me, I looked the other way. I wasn't going to get into a confrontation for Chiffon. I wasn't security, so I didn't bother. When you treat people like shit, they will not go the extra mile for you or for the company.

Dennis was one of the designers. One day he brought into work those little firecracker poppers that are rolled into white tissue. When you throw them onto something hard, they pop. People use them on the Fourth of July.

The copier was near my desk, so anyone making copies would stop and chat with me. We would talk shit about work and Cindy; everyone hated her. Dennis and I waited for one of his assistants to go to the copier. Before she started making copies, we threw a few poppers at the wall to scare her. She screamed so loudly that all the other employees came out of their offices to see what was going on. Dennis and I almost peed in our pants from laughing. Cindy was not happy at all and gave us a dirty look.

Later on that day, Cindy called me into her office. I knew that was the end for me.

"Please sit, and close the door," she said with a smile.

Yup, I was going to get the ax. "What's up?"

"Well…this is not going to work out. We have to let you go."

"OK," I said.

She handed me an envelope. "This is your—"

"Don't bother," I said, cutting her off. "You know, people kill other people in offices because of people like you."

Cindy turned pale, and I walked out. I'm happy it is over. This was a long year working here. I decided to change the interview suit a bit. I wore a black top with the red skirt and open toe black pantent shoe. A month later I found another job.

Four

IVAN MANDEL

Ivan Mandel was the hottest up-and-coming designer around. He had started his company in the late '80s and blew up in the '90s. He was not afraid of any hemline and dared to do it all, from his colorful fur coats to his dangerous backdrop gowns.

It had all started with two friends: Ivan Mandel and Sally Hyme. They had met at a bar mitzvah. Now their office was in SoHo, and it was very small. We all sat together; there was just no room. My desk was a file cabinet.

Sally Hyme was a wonderful person and a kind woman—which I found to be very rare in the business. She had made the first samples for the line and put up the money to start the business. Buyers had taken one look at the line, and they were sold. They loved it. Word spread like wildfire, and the business took off.

As the company grew, we had to move. Four months after I started, we occupied an entire loft building with several floors. It was such a change from Midtown, with all those savages on the street and those rolling carts.

It was great. Everything was new: desks, computers—whatever we wanted we got. There was a kitchen fully stocked with coffee, juice, soda, and popcorn, and there was a washer and dryer. The best part of it was that my boss was a man, gay, and fabulous. He spoiled all of the girls in the office, but we worked very hard. I was finally home.

Spring Show

I wasn't participating in the show, but I was in the audience, which was better. First I went in the back to check out what was going on. The show was held in our new building. It was my first real fashion show. All the top models were there: Naomi Campbell, Cindy Crawford, Linda Evangelista, and more. I couldn't believe my eyes, but I was not model-struck. I was just excited to be here.

The models were getting their hair and makeup done by Kevin Aucoin and Sam Fine. These guys were amazing makeup artist. The dressers were looking at their board with the changes for their models. It was amazing.

Once Ivan said, "Let's get ready," they all got into their positions, and I went to see the show.

Of course it was standing room only. All of the seats were for buyers, celebrities, and press, but from where I was standing I could see everything. It got really dark, and then the lights on the stage went on, and so did the music. The models started walking onto the runway. First was Naomi Campbell and then Christy Turlington, Cindy Crawford and Linda Evangelista. They didn't stop. It was one famous model after another. Oh my God!

The clothes were all fabulous. There were sequined gowns in pink, blue, and orange, with fur coats to match. They were to die for. I was in love. It was not what I had expected, but I hadn't known what to expect. The dresses, the jackets, the shoes, and the bags were for spring. I wanted everything. The colors were beautiful, and based on the applause, the buyers loved it all too.

I hadn't realized how big Ivan was until that show. At the end of the show, Ivan has his favorite model Melanie came out in a wedding gown. Melanie was tall and beautiful, she had carmel skin and green eyes. She was very nice. The other models followed and made room for Ivan to walk through while everyone applauded. It was amazing that it had taken months of preparation to create a half-hour show.

There had been so much going on before the show took place too. While we were showing the spring line, the fall line was being shipped.

I was glad I wasn't a receptionist anymore. Not that there was anything wrong with it, but I was bored, and I wanted more. I had been hired to enter orders and ship them even though I had never done that before, but they saw my passion. I was getting a $5,000 clothing allowance for each season with a 40 percent discount on top of that. My boss was Michael.

Michael Green was very pleasant and soft spoken. He was gay and wonderful. He had been with the company for a year. He was the vice president of sales.

I was very busy shipping to all of the major stores: Bergdorf Goodman, Neiman Marcus, Barneys, and Saks, to name a few. During crunch time everyone stayed in, and the company paid for lunch. We had the best lunches: Jerry's, Dean and Deluca, and Olives.

Things were going amazingly well. I loved going to work. Michael was the best. He never yelled or got mad. Once a week we sat together to work on delivery dates and items that were shipping out. I would create pick tickets, coordinate with the warehouse to ship items to the stores. It made it so easy when the warehouse was in the same building.

The morning after the show, Ivan picked up *Women's Wear Daily* to see the reviews. We were all on pins and needles, waiting to read the review. Everyone was invited to the showroom for a viewing of the show on video and to eat pizza. It was a great review and Ivan was happy.

Ivan began creating the next fall line and making the sketches come to life. As the months passed, samples were getting made. The spring line had been amazing. I couldn't image what the fall line would look like.

Six months later we were showing the fall line in the tents at Bryant Park. The show started at 3:00 p.m., but everyone working had to be there by 11:00 a.m. to set up everything. Everyone who was working the show had to wear a white shirt and black pants.

It was so crowded. Security was all over the place. People were outside, waiting to get in. Some would even counterfeit the invitations to get peeks at the collection. Public relations staff members were at the door. I just walked in. I felt like a celebrity.

I had been chosen to be one of the dressers, which meant I would be dressing one of the supermodels. I wasn't scared—more like nervous. And I was so excited because it was the first time I'd be dressing at a show. I was surprised that Ivan Mandel picked me to dress. I wondered who I would be dressing.

While the public relations staff worked on the stage and the seating arrangements, the rest of us were in the back, removing the plastic bags from the clothes that were on the racks. When I arrived at my rack, the first thing I did was check who I was dressing.

Oh my God! Cindy Crawford. I was going to dress Cindy Crawford. That was big. I loved my job!

I had to study the Polaroid pictures that were attached to a whiteboard hung on the rack. I had to make sure all accessories and shoes were lined up with the garments shown in the pictures. All the shoes had to be scraped on the bottom to avoid slipping on the runway. There would be times when we would have to switch accessories or shoes with a model after she walked the runaway. I had to get accessories and shoes from two different models, which scared me because they had to be right. I had to get a bracelet from Linda Evangelista and shoes from Naomi Campbell. When a model would come in from the runway, she would run to the rack and take off her clothes and shoes really fast. I had to have the next outfit ready, help her with her shoes, and get the accessories or shoes I needed from another model so she could go on next. There were fifteen models, and they had five changes each.

We were hanging around, and waiting for the models and the food to arrive. After I checked my rack, I walked over to Julie to see who she was dressing.

Julie Camacho was our receptionist. She was Puerto Rican from Brooklyn, five feet eight inches, with light skin and long, wavy hair. When I first met Julie, it was like we'd known each other for years—maybe from a past life. We immediately clicked and became good friends. Julie had been with the company for a year.

Before Julie was hired, we had gone through several receptionists. There had been one who was nosy and snobbish. The last one had never been at her desk. The phone would ring three to four times before she picked up. Because of the way our offices were set up—the receptionist's desk was out front, and everyone was stationed behind a wall with a few entrances—we all knew when she was not there. We would purposely call the front desk as if we were people calling from outside. When she would run back to her desk, we would hang up. We entertained ourselves that way until she was gone. Then finally they hired Julie.

"Hey, Julie."

She was on the floor, scraping the bottoms of some shoes. She looked up and said, "Hey."

I pointed at the whiteboard. "I need that gold bracelet after Linda finishes."

"OK," she said. "Who are you dressing?"

"Cindy Crawford! Can you believe it? I'm glad I didn't get Naomi."

"I know. Me too. I heard Cindy is really nice."

"I hope so," I said.

"Linda is nice too, and she's so beautiful. Were both lucky to be dressing nice models, but I'm sure the next show we won't be so lucky."

We both chuckled.

Denise walked over to us. "What the hell are you guys laughing about?" she asked.

Denise Gill had been with the company for six months. She worked for the production department. Denise sourced everything and anything for each garment. It was a very stressful position, but she was good at her job. She was from Harlem, Puerto Rican and Black, with beautiful, caramel-colored skin. Denise was five feet, ten inches tall and had freckles and curly hair. We clicked immediately. I think it was the freckles, which we both had.

Julie and I stopped laughing.

"Who are you dressing?" I asked.

"Naomi Campbell, man!" Denise said with a smirk.

"Aw, damn! Oh, by the way, I need those black leather boots after Naomi finishes. OK?"

"Yeah, whatever," Denise said.

Julie and I looked at each other, our eyes opened wide. Naomi Campbell was difficult to work with. Some of the supermodels thought they could step on people, and no one would say anything. Not Denise, she didn't care. She would fight Naomi.

As the models started to arrive, Cindy Crawford entered. She had no makeup on, and she was still beautiful. Thank God I was not model crazy because they were all there: Naomi Campbell, Cindy Turlington, Cindy Crawford, Kate Moss, Linda Evangelista, and Veronica Webb. I couldn't believe they were all there in my face. As they were getting their hair and makeup done, I was getting nervous. I was about to dress a supermodel. Oh my God! But you know, they were women just like me, but a lot taller and thinner and with bigger bank accounts.

They smoked cigarettes and drank Diet Coke all day. There was one particular model who would always have a bottle of liquor in her purse. The food was just for show. The models never touched it, so the rest of us ate it.

After hair and makeup were done, Cindy Crawford walked toward my rack. I waved to her. She smiled, and I smiled.

"Hi," I said.

"Hi, I'm Cindy."

"I know, and I love you."

"Thanks," she said with a smile.

I felt like a nerd saying hello to the popular girl.

Ivan yelled, "Girls, get in your first looks!"

And from then on he requested that I dress the models during the shows. I was really happy there.

Ivan added a new model to his favorites list: Tyra Banks. There was one show when Tyra was walking the runway, and she was working it. It looked like Naomi Campbell was not happy about something. I heard that Naomi and Tyra were not friends. Naomi had every reason to worry: Tyra was younger and beautiful, and she owned that runway.

There were times when we had a demand for a certain size or a special order, and if we didn't have the size we would change the label. If the special order required a size six, we would send a size eight with a size six label. The customer would think she was losing weight. The customers were happy, so we were happy. It may have been wrong, but it was just business.

During one market week, there was a lot of running around. Everyone seemed frantic, from the flower deliverers to the caterers. I had no clue what was going on until this woman walked into the office with a perfect bob and no hair out of place and wearing a Chanel suit, purse, shoes, and shades. It was Anna Wintour, the editor of *Vogue*, the magazine of all fashion. If she approved your line, you were in, and she loved Ivan. She featured him on the cover of *Vogue's* fall couture issue. It was amazing how people reacted to her because of a title she held. I guess that's fashion for you.

Fashion Week was here again. I had been there for two years already. We were showing the fall line. The showroom was always freezing while showing the fall line because it made the buyers buy more coats.

One afternoon I noticed that everyone had gone to lunch with Ivan, but they hadn't invited me. My feelings were hurt, but I got over it. I didn't like it, but I didn't say anything.

During our Christmas party I was at the bar with Lee.

When I'd first met Lee Cruz, she had just come back from the island of Jamaica. Damn! She had a tan only the Caribbean could give you. It was like dark chocolate. Only her eyes and her teeth were white. Lee was the fabric buyer. She was good at it; she knew her job. We also clicked immediately.

We were having another drink and feeling good, when Ivan walked by. I grabbed his shirt with my fist and said, "Yeah, the next time you take the whole floor out and don't tell me, you're in trouble."

He was so stunned that all he said was, "OK."

I laughed. "Merry Christmas."

We hugged.

"Merry Christmas, Anita," Ivan said.

Meanwhile Lee had her mouth wide open from shock over what I had just did. Then we both burst out laughing.

"Oh my God," she said. "What the hell, Anita?" Then she fell off her bar stool, and we couldn't stop laughing.

Denise and Julie walks over to Lee and I.

"Hey guys", said Denise

"We came just in time", said Julie

"What do you mean?", I asked

"Ivan, he smells like salami", said Julie

We were all hysterically laughing.

Then I stopped laughing and I said, "Really?"

"Oh yes he does", said Julie

I looked at Lee and I said, "He does?"

"Yeah, he does."

"Now I'm afraid to be near him because I'm going to sniff him."

We all laughed so hard we were crying.

That same Christmas someone sent Ivan several boxes in gift wrap. When he opened them, his clothes were inside. One of the accounts had sent back merchandise. That account had wanted to return the merchandise, but we'd told them it was past ninety days. Now we were forced to take it back.

Year after year, things were great. I was wearing the hottest designer clothing, and I was making money. I designed handbags part-time and sold to several boutiques in SoHo. I would like to start my own handbag line.

Ivan decided to add a secondary line, but things started to change. The line was more affordable. What were not affordable were the department's salaries. They were outrageous. It was insulting to the rest of us. Someone put envelopes in our mailboxes with information about everyone's salaries in the new division. We never found out who did it, but we were all pissed. Our production assistant's salary was $35,000, and the other division's production assistant's salary was $65,000.

The couture line was doing well, but who knew how the secondary line would do. Another company had purchased Ivan's name, and that was why they were trying the affordable line. The changes were coming fast because Sally Hyme left the company. We all cried when she left. As the company grew, so did Ivan's ego.

Ivan and the president, Glen White, were having issues regarding the new line. They exchanged words, and their relationship soured. They had been goods friends before they worked with each other.

Glen had been with the company since day one. He was the president of the company and a wonderful boss. He was very respectful and never micro managed.

Several months after Sally Hyme resign, Glen resigned. That Friday we all cried again and said good-bye to Glen. The following Monday morning, we all met the new president: Heather Smith.

Heather was a thin, frail, bowlegged woman with mousy-brown, shoulder-length hair. She always wore a suit jacket with leggings. It was not attractive, especially with her bowed legs.

Almost every afternoon Julie would make popcorn and share it with us. Michael and Glen had spoiled everyone with a stocked fridge. One afternoon Denise and I were chatting with Julie while eating popcorn at the front desk. When Heather walked in at 1:00 p.m., we all said good afternoon. Then, without asking, Heather grabbed a handful of popcorn and walked away.

We all looked at each other. What the hell just happened? Our eyes opened wide. We couldn't believe it.

"What the hell was that?" Denise asked.

I said, "That was rude. I bet if anyone of us had done that to her, she wouldn't have liked it."

"Bitch," Julie said.

"That's our president," I said.

We laughed.

Everyone had to attend a meeting about the new line and the new changes. Heather was standing next to me as everyone was gathering. I noticed she was biting her nails. It looked like she had warts on her fingers. I couldn't stop looking at them. They were disgusting.

Heather spoke: "Hi, everyone, and thanks for coming. I'm going to keep this short. As you know there are several employees who are no longer with us. We are happy you are here with us today. We are moving forward with the secondary line, and there will be many changes. This is a good thing for the company. I will keep everyone posted. Thank you."

Walking out of the room, I could feel the tension in the air. Everyone from the secondary line was all smiles. The rest of us weren't.

While I was in the kitchen, eating popcorn, Heather walked in.

"Hi, everyone. Denise, thanks for the report," she said.

"Sure," Denise said.

Heather made a cup of coffee, ripped a sugar packet open, used only half, and then put the rest of the packet back into the basket. She again grabbed a handful of popcorn from the bag I was holding.

"Oh please, take it. I'm stuffed," I said.

With no clue Heather took the popcorn bag and smiled. "Thanks," she said and then walked away.

Denise shoved me. "Why did you let her take the popcorn? It was the last bag we had."

I looked out of the kitchen door to make sure Heather was not around. "Let me see. Hmm…warts or no popcorn? She has warts on her fingers, and now I know she's the one who takes half the sugar in a packet and puts it back. No one wants an open pack of sugar."

"Yuck!"

"Didn't you see them?"

Julie's face was red. I was laughing hysterically.

"You're lying," Julie said.

"I swear, Julie. Didn't you see her biting her nails in the meeting?" I asked.

"No."

Denise said, "I did!

"She was standing next to me, and I saw the warts. When you see her, check out her fingers."

Heather sent out a memo regarding how our company and many other companies were expanding. We all laughed because it was confusing and had so many typos. She spelled Chanel "Channel." Heather was not smart, and we all wondered how she had gotten so far. She was clueless. A nitwit.

"She's not smart at all," Julie said.

I said, "Thank God she's not the president of the United States."

"We would all be in trouble," Denise said.

We all laughed.

Michael couldn't stand Heather. I was afraid he would leave too. Several months later he resigned. The company hired Patty Palmer to replace Michael.

Patty Palmer was from London and seemed nice. She was very pale, with blond hair and freckles. I liked her, and we worked well together, but there were more changes to come. There was no more space in the warehouse. There were more units for the secondary line than the couture line. We needed more space—a lot more space.

My phone rang. "Hello," I said.

"Hi, Anita, it's Patty. Can you come down to my office?"

"Sure, I'll be right over." Every time I'd heard those words, it had never been good. Shit, was I getting fired? The way things were going at the company, I wouldn't doubt it.

I walked into Patty's office.

"Hi, Anita, please sit," she said.

"So, what's going on?" I asked.

Patty broke the news to me. My heart dropped. "The warehouse is moving to Secaucus, New Jersey."

"Am I going too?" I asked with a worried look on my face.

She paused and then said, "Yes."

I closed my eyes like I was in pain. "Damn, but why?"

"As you know we are expanding, and we need more room," Patty said.

Yeah, more room for the new, expensive division, I thought.

"But can't I work from here?" I asked.

"No, I'm sorry."

I sighed. "OK. I'll see you later."

I was so pissed. Now I had to commute to Jersey. I sighed all day.

A few months later, the company hired another person to run the warehouse. Now, that really pissed me off, because after working there for five years, they should have considered me. Now I have to show her the ropes.

I knew my days were numbered, and I would be looking for another job.

Dana Patelli was the warehouse manager. My new boss. I already didn't like her. She had a manly walk; it was like a strut. I knew there would be trouble, and I would get fired. I really had a hard time with me working here in New Jersey and Patty knew it.

It was hard for me to teach Dana my job, but I didn't show her everything. Let her figure it out for herself.

While we were in a meeting, discussing sales, shipping, and production, Patty asked, "Anita, are we on time with everything?"

"Yes, except Bergdorf Goodman. I'm still waiting for the jackets to come in before I ship the pants."

"OK, we—"

"Why are you not shipping the pants?" Dana interrupted.

"Because—" I began.

"Why, Anita? Why?" she interrupted me.

I gave her a dirty look.

"Well, I'm sure Anita can explain if you stop interrupting everyone. Then you would know the bloody answer," Patty said. Her face was all red, and she was pissed.

I just smiled at Patty and gave Dana the evil eye. She was a nitwit.

"Thank you, Patty," I said. "The start date is in two weeks. The jackets will be here this week or early next week, in time to ship with the pants. We are shipping them together because their PO states to ship them together. Because their ads are dropping in two weeks."

"You're welcome, Anita. Dana, please learn to read the POs so there isn't any confusion."

"OK," Dana said. She was pissed, and I didn't care. She deserved it.

Working in Secaucus was not working for me. Though the company paid for my commute, I was still not happy. I had to be at Port Authority at 7:15 a.m. to catch a bus to make it to Secaucus by 8:30 a.m. If I missed the bus, it was guaranteed I would be late. It had been hard getting to work by 9:00 a.m. in New York. Imagine trying to get to Jersey by 8:30 a.m. And to make things worse, the walk from the bus stop to the warehouse was half a mile. It just kept getting worse.

What sealed the deal was where I was sitting. All of my stuff had been shipped to the new warehouse. There were two small offices and three desks outside the offices. I knew I was not getting an office. I was sure I would be sitting at one of the three desks. And sure enough, when I arrived all my stuff was near one of them.

I had a beat-up wooden desk with roaches all over the place and a terminal—not a PC, a terminal with an amber-colored screen. I was livid. And things just got worse.

The two other desks were for Jennifer and Stacey.

Jennifer had recently started working for the company. She lived in the Bronx. She had been hired to enter orders.

Stacey was also new. She had been hired to handle credits and returns. She lived in Queens. We all traveled together to and from Jersey.

The bell rang. It was lunchtime. The girls and I went to the lunch cart outside.

"What's going on, Anita?" Jennifer asked.

"Well, I worked in the SoHo office for five years, and now they dumped me here with this bitch as my boss."

Stacey said, "Damn, I'm sorry."

"Yeah, I am too."

Jennifer said, "She looks like a bitch."

"Yup, yup," Stacy said.

Every day I would show up to work with a heavy sigh and so unhappy. Every day Dana would ask me to show her what I did again. I showed her only half of what I did. I knew where things were going. It was not going to end well.

Dana and Cary were getting the offices. Cary was new. It was terrible, but at that point I was not going to fight a battle I was losing.

Cary was new to the company. I didn't know what her job title was, and I didn't care.

Joe was the floor supervisor of the warehouse. Every time I asked him a question, he would end his answer with "super." Everything was super.

While I was looking for something on my desk, Joe slowly approached me. He was very annoying and smelled like urine. He was always upstairs in the office instead of on the warehouse floor, where he belonged.

"How do you work with your desk a mess?" he asked.

"What?" I asked as I turned around.

"How do you work with that mess on your desk?"

I gave him the evil eye. "I know where everything is. Can I help you with something?"

"No, everything is super," Joe said with his thumbs up.

Under my breath I said, "Then super your ass out my face." I didn't even bother to look up. I continued my search for a routing guide.

The next morning Dana walked over to my desk. While pointing to my desk, she said, "I want to see what's on your desk."

"What?"

She raised her voice at me and started pounding her finger hard on my desk. "I said I want to know what's on your desk."

Jennifer and Stacey looked at me, and I looked at them. They shook their heads like that wasn't right. I opened my eyes as if to say, "See what I mean?"

"What are you looking for?" I asked.

"Neiman Marcus order."

I looked through some papers and pulled a file and gave it to her. "Here."

"Now I want to see what's on your desk."

"No," I said.

"Excuse me?"

"I said no. Why do you need to see what's on my desk? I get the job done, which is more important than what is on my desk. Plus this is how I have always worked." It was an organized mess, and I knew where everything was. That little piece of shit Joe had told her.

Dana walked away pissed. I immediately called Patty.

"Anita, how are you?" she asked.

"Not good. I'm not happy here. Dana is giving me a hard time."

"What do you mean?"

"She wants to inspect what's on my desk," I said.

"What do you mean inspect what's on your desk?"

"Patty, she wants to go through it. She wants to know about every piece of paper on my desk. It's none of her business, and I told her no."

"OK. I will talk to her."

Patty did nothing to help me. The company had shipped me to Secaucus, and that was it. They didn't care. They washed their hands of me. I was on my own. Julie and Denise were so pissed, but they couldn't do anything either. Sigh.

That year we had sixteen snowstorms. One morning the sun was shining, but it started to snow around ten o'clock, and it looked like a blizzard by eleven thirty. The company decided to close the warehouse early, and when Stacey and I went outside it was snowing hard and we were unable to see. We put our shades on so we can see and held on to each other because it was windy. We were walking blind. Lucky for Jennifer she'd called in sick.

It took us about forty-five minutes to walk that half a mile to the bus stop. It was cold and windy, and the bus was taking forever. After we'd stood there for about two hours, Cary passed by in her Pathfinder. She looked our way and shrugged her shoulders as if to say sorry and kept on driving. I was so pissed because she could have taken us to a train station instead of leaving us to wait in that blizzard. I couldn't believe she had done that. But she would pay for it.

On Monday morning I was on a mission.

I said to Jennifer, "Come with me. Stacey, you watch out for Dana and Cary. Stacey, she will pay for what she did to us."

"What are you going to do?" Stacy asked.

"Don't worry. Just watch out for us."

"OK."

Jennifer and I walked toward the door.

"What's up?" Jennifer asked.

"I need you to stay here and watch my back," I said.

"OK."

A few minutes later, we walked back into the office.

Dana and Cary were leaving. Dana said to Stacey, "We're both going to lunch. We'll see you later."

"OK," Stacy said.

Ten minutes later Cary came running into the office. "I have to call a tow truck. I have four flat tires."

Stacey and Jennifer looked at me and smiled.

I winked at them.

—⟋⟍—

Dana was constantly on my back about my desk and what I was doing. She had nothing better to do than harass me. It got to the point that I lost respect for her.

"I want to see what's on your desk," she said.

"No. Anything you need to know, just ask me," I said. While she was speaking to me, I looked the other way.

"There could be things there that have not been shipped, and you're holding them on your desk."

"There's nothing that's pending on my desk. Everything is up to date. You can always run a report and see if anything is still pending. You know how to do that, right?"

"Come to my office," Dana said.

After we walked into her office, Dana closed the door. "Please sit," she said.

"No, I'd rather stand," I said.

"I don't like your attitude."

"I have done nothing wrong. You're harassing me, and I don't like it."

"If you don't like it, you can find another job," Dana said.

"If you don't like it, fire me."

Two weeks later I was fired.

While I was packing my desk, my phone rang, but I didn't answer it. Dana was standing over me.

"Why are you standing here?" I asked. "Don't worry, I'm not going to steal or delete anything."

"I'm supposed to stand here," she said.

"Whatever." I continued to pack. The phone rang again, and I picked it up. "What?"

"What's wrong?"

"Who's this?"

"It's us, Denise and Julie. What the hell is going on?"

"I was fired, and I'm packing my shit. This one over here"—I pointed at Dana—"is watching me to make sure I don't steal anything. Like anything here is worth taking. Bye, guys. I'll call you later."

"We love you."

"Love you guys too."

While all of that was going on, Jennifer and Stacey were witnessing it. I stood up and grabbed my purse.

"Peace out, girls, and good luck here. This company will be closed soon," I said.

I would miss working with them. We waved at each other, and I left the building. I did a lot of thinking on that last half-mile walk to the bus stop. It was March 20, a cold day. It felt good to walk. I didn't even feel a thing. I was just beaten and tired of the job. I had no idea when the bus was coming. I had no idea how long I'd been waiting, but it had been a while. I thought about how I had been thrown to the wolves. I would find something else, like I always did. I will keep designing my handbags and see what happens. I looked down the street, and the bus was coming. Hallelujah.

After a year the secondary line bankrupted the company. They failed on the quality of the goods. The line got bad review after bad review. A year later Ivan Mandel closed the company.

Five

NINA SANCHEZ

After Ivan Mandel I didn't think I could find another job right away with nice people.

Nina Sanchez was a woman's shoe company. Nina was the designer, and everything was manufactured in Spain. They had their own factories and offices in Spain and New York. Pedro Sanchez was Nina's father, and he ran the New York City office ,but from Spain.

Pedro Sanchez had invested in his daughter's dream, and they were doing very well. Pedro came to New York and Vegas two times a year. He loved shopping at Conway's.

My interview was with Linda Rodriguez, who hired me right on the spot. I wore my red interview jacket with black skirt and up to the knee leather boots.

The New York offices were in the Cotton Incorporated building at Fifty-Sixth Street and Sixth Avenue. Linda was looking for an administrative assistant. It would be nice to work for a shoe company, I love shoes, but what girl doesn't? It was a nice change since they were from Spain. There were so many shoe companies in the building. Every Thursday we had customers come to shop and order shoes.

Linda Rodriquez had been with Nina Sanchez for more than ten years. She ran the New York Office and was the salesperson for the major New York department stores. She was a beautiful Puerto Rican woman in her fifties with style and a major attitude. She lived on Central Park West. Linda looked expensive and shopped expensive. She had even been featured on Oprah, on a show about women who overspent.

We got along as long as I got to work on time and didn't make any personal calls. There were several times I was a few minutes late—I got in at 9:03 a.m.—and when I walked in the office Linda looked at her watch. She never said anything, but I saw her looking. So I made it a point never to be late. There were times my girlfriends would call, and I would pretend someone was calling about our sample sale because Linda's desk was across from mine, so I could never talk.

We worked well together. Once Linda was going on vacation to Italy, so I had to make sure I could run the office while she was away. I was happy she was going because it meant I would be in the office by myself, plus I would get more work done.

The week that Linda was on vacation was great, and I ran the office with no problems. After her vacation she got into the office before I did.

"Good morning, Anita," she said.

She was tanned and looked rich and was smiling from ear to ear. She was in a good mood.

"Good morning, Linda. How was your vacation?" I asked.

"It was wonderful. I met a wonderful man, and I'm in love. We're getting married."

"Wow! That's wonderful news."

"And the best part is I'm moving to Italy," she said.

"No way."

"Yes!"

She got up, and we hugged.

"This is just wonderful. Congratulations," I said.

"Thank you."

I think I was happier for myself because it meant I would be running the office. Congratulations to me. Don't get me wrong, she was nice, and we got along, but working with another woman in those close quarters…nah. I'd rather be by myself. I could happily do my job and go home.

Linda was marrying a rich dentist who lived in Sicily; he owned a mansion overlooking the Mediterranean Sea and an apartment in the city. She was also keeping her Central Park West apartment. Plus she wouldn't have to work. She was having two receptions: one in the Hamptons and the second in Italy.

I attended her wedding in the Hamptons. It was beautiful. She was a gorgeous bride. It was held in a mansion right on the beach that belonged to one of her girlfriends. The mansion had been featured in *Hamptons Magazine*. I wanted a house like that one someday.

After Linda left the company, things were great, even though sometimes I felt lonely. But I got over it real fast. It made me think about how awful people behaved because of their titles. They were probably miserable at home and needed to release their frustration on their employees.

Pedro was in town for the New York shoe show. He would only stay for a week or two. He was always in the office when I arrived. I could smell the coffee he brewed fresh. He worked with the sales reps and customers all day while I did my job. I loved the company, and Pedro never yelled at me.

I had time to work on designing my handbags. I sold to several stores and was working on more. I was working with a manufacturer in Brooklyn.

Kevin Charles sold to all the mom-and-pop stores. When Linda left the company, he took over the major department stores. He had been with Nancy Sanchez for five years and in the industry for more than twenty-five years. Kevin was married with children. He was good to work with, and he wasn't rude. I always helped him pack the shoes for shows.

I was able to order any shoes I wanted, and I didn't have to pay for them. Too bad I was not the sample size, which was seven, because I would have needed an apartment just for the shoes.

I learned a lot about the shoe business and the hard work and money it took to start a shoe company or any company.

—————

Business was great and everyone was happy. I had been with Nina Sanchez for two years. I was making good money, and the bonuses were good. I saved a lot of it because I wanted to have my own business one day.

The next year business slowed down. Sales weren't good. There was not enough to support the New York office and my salary, though the company was profiting nicely in Europe.

Pedro sat me down and told me he would be closing the office at the end of the year. He gave me enough time to start looking for another job and allowed me to go on interviews. I was so upset, but I understood.

When he was in the office for the shoe show, exactly at 3:00 p.m. he would ask, *"Se va a hacer el café?"*

"Si," I said.

I didn't have to deal with too many other people, but there I was again, looking for another job. It was on my terms...well, not really. It was like getting fired.

Every day I searched *Women's Wear Daily* for a job. I found an ad for a customer-service manager at Franco Giovanni. I faxed over my résumé, and someone called me immediately to set up an interview.

Franco Giovanni was a famous designer. The position would look good on my résumé. I hadn't thought I was going to get a response right away since it was a day before Christmas Eve. I was a bit surprised; it was happening kind of quick. Maybe I wasn't ready, but in reality

I had no choice. Nina Sanchez was closing. After the interview I got another call from Franco Giovanni's Human Resources department, and I got the job. I wore a black two button blazer with the red skirt and black leather stilettos.

I still went in to the Nina Sanchez office once a week for an hour to get the mail, pay some bills, and balance out the checking account. Two years later Kevin and I cleaned the office out and turned off the lights.

Six

FRANCO GIOVANNI

I couldn't believe I'd landed a job at Franco Giovanni on Christmas Eve. Merry Christmas to me.

Franco Giovanni had been on the fashion map for more than fifteen years. He had been designer of the year for five years in a row. He was known for his elegant dresses and tailored men's suits made from the finest Italian fabrics. He lived and worked in Italy. The New York office was on Forty-Second Street and Fifth Avenue. The office was so white and clean—never mind the showrooms. They were just so beautiful, I was afraid to touch anything. There were mahogany tables and shelves trimmed in handcrafted flowers. All the chairs were covered in white suede, and the rugs were so plush I just wanted to sleep on them.

As the new customer-service manager, I would be managing a staff of five. I received a $5,000 clothing allowance each year after my 40 percent off and a discount card for all the flagship stores around the world. The job would look good on my résumé, but it seemed too good to be true.

Stephen Lowe was my boss and the vice president of sales. He'd been with the company for more than two years.

When I first arrived, Stephen walked me around the office. Everyone was so nice, and I noticed that all the notebooks on the shelves were black and only black. There wasn't a colored notebook in sight. Almost everyone wore black in the office. It was great for me because I loved wearing black. It was classy, clean, and made me like thinner.

Past the reception area to the right was an enormous, long closet where everyone hung their coats, umbrellas, and stuff. It was a dream closet. They also had two kitchens that were fully stocked with juice, soda, hot chocolate, coffee, popcorn, and other stuff. There was a sign on the microwave that said: "PLEASE DON'T BURN THE POPCORN. THREE MINUTES!"

The reception area was all white: white walls, white furniture, and a white receptionist—Stacey, who was a bit spacey. She had blue eyes and blond hair she wore in a high ponytail, so when she walked and talked it swung from side to side. She would greet everyone with a smile and her swinging ponytail.

When passing some of my coworkers, I felt that most of them seemed nice, but for some reason I felt like I was in the *Stepford Wives* movie. They were happy in a phony way. It seemed like their smiles were forced.

All the girls were in the conference room when Stephen and I walked in.

"Hi, girls. This is Anita. She's our new customer-service manager," he said.

Everyone said hi. I noticed one girl already had an attitude. She had her lips pressed together. I said to myself, *This one will be a problem.*

The girls I would be managing seemed normal, but they were young and very immature. Saundra, who did all the order entries, was very nice to me. She helped me get all of my office supplies and got me settled in. Sophie, Jeannette, and Laura were all sales assistants. They were a little clique. They ate lunch together and worked together. They were like a school of fish. And then there was Joann. She did all the preshipping and allocations. She gave me attitude when I first arrived.

Once I sent an e-mail out about a 10:00 a.m. meeting. Everyone arrived on time except for Joann. Fifteen minutes later she walked in, and the little clique giggled like high school girls.

"Settle down, girls," I said. "We can now start the meeting. Joann, did you get my e-mail that this meeting was at ten o'clock?"

"Yes," Joann said.

The girls giggled again. I gave them a look, and they stopped.

"This is just a brief meeting to get myself familiar with everyone's responsibilities. Also, please be on time for future meetings. Thank you."

I scheduled a meeting every Monday at 10:00 a.m. I wanted to see if the little bitch would be late. Sure enough, she was late each time, and she made it into a joke.

After one meeting I was walking to my desk, and I heard someone call my name.

I turned around. It was Saundra.

"Hey," I said.

"I just want to speak with you privately," Saundra said.

"Sure. What's going on?"

"I noticed you looking at Joann with an attitude."

"Yes, I did."

"Well, she's mad because they didn't give her your position," Saundra said.

"Well, that's not my fault. She should be mad at whoever didn't give her the position."

"That's what I told her, girl."

"Thank you," I said.

"Sure, girl; anytime."

They had hired me to manage that group, and that was what I was going to do.

After the third meeting, while everyone was leaving, I asked Joann, "Can you stay for a minute?"

"Sure," she said.

I looked straight into her eyes, but she stared at the wall. "Joann, I'm trying to work with you, and you are not cooperating. We can work together and make this work."

She continued to look at the wall and even did that with an attitude. "Well, I don't need you to make this work. I have been making it work since way before you got here. I've been here for more than eight years, and I know what I'm doing. It should have been me."

"I totally understand your position, but you should be upset at whoever hired me. I have no fault in this."

She sat there with her lips pressed tightly together and her arms crossed over her chest. "Are we done?"

I smirked. "We are now."

It was not going to work and I really didn't feel like babysitting. But that was nothing new in the industry, huh?

—◌ɱ◌—

I'd had enough after several months of putting in ten-hour days, trying to get a project done for a meeting scheduled in two days. I shut down my computer, and I was out. As I was passing Stephen's office, I overheard him and Adam in a heated argument over something. Apparently Stephen and Adam were lovers, and no one knew. Stephen was married with children, and Adam was single and waiting for Stephen to leave his wife for him. Every time I saw Stephen, he reminded me of a Cabbage Patch doll.

I heard Adam yelling. "You want me anytime, anywhere you want, and now you can't spend time with me? What the hell is going on?"

"Shut up! Someone's going to hear you."

"I don't fucking care. Let everyone hear it!"

"It's over, Adam. I don't want this anymore."

As soon as I was about to turn the corner, I saw Stephen's office door open. I turned the corner and walked as fast as I could to the closet to get my coat.

The next morning I worked on the report I was putting together for Stephen's big meeting. Finally it was done, and I was happy that I would be able to leave the office on time. Then I checked the report against the system and found the report was incorrect. The numbers were all wrong.

"Shit, shit, shit. Oh, boy. Why is this wrong? I'm screwed."

I was so confused because the information was based on what Joann had given me. Of course, Joann! She'd screwed me over. That little bitch had given me the wrong information.

Stephen was coming out of his meeting.

"Hey, Stephen, I need to speak to you when you get a chance," I said.

"Yes, you do!" he said with an attitude.

That didn't sound right. Something was wrong. I was probably going to get fired.

Several days later I had a meeting with Stephen. We spoke about how things were going and how the girls were doing.

"So, what's going on, Anita?" he asked.

"Everyone is cooperating except Joann. She seems mad. She told me she knows her job and that she's been doing it for eight years."

"You know she's my protégé, right?" Stephen asked.

I smiled. "No, I didn't know. Why wasn't she given this position?"

"She was not ready."

"She's not happy, and she's taking it out on me. Also the numbers she gave me for the reports were not correct."

"Let me see what I can do. I'll speak to Joann. Also this is the third report you gave me that's incorrect," Stephen said.

"Why are you telling me now?"

"I didn't realize it until Adam bitched about it, but then Joann gave me a corrected one."

"Really? She never told me, and FYI, I got the information from her."

"OK. Thanks," Stephen said.

I stood up and walked away. Why should I be surprised? It seemed to be the nature of the business—what comes around goes around.

That afternoon the clique, Stacey, and Joann were all out to lunch. I found that strange because there was always someone in the office. Stephen called me into his office. I knew what was coming.

"Please sit," he said.

"What's up?" I asked.

"You know the reports you gave me were not correct?"

The reports—the fucking reports. That was all he had.

"Yes, I know. We spoke about it. I also told you Joann gave me the numbers, and that's how I created the reports."

"Yes, I know. I'm sorry to say this, but we have to let you go," Stephen said.

"Why?" I asked.

"We decided to eliminate the position."

My eyes got watery. I felt very emotional because I had really tried to make it work.

"Please," Stephen said, "this has nothing to do with you. We are downsizing."

"OK, you're downsizing. But you keep saying it's the reports. What's up with that? You know what? Never mind." I got up and snatched the envelope from his hand.

"Can you leave your ID?" he asked.

I threw my ID on his desk.

"Good luck," Stephen said.

I walked out.

Oh my God, there I was again. I grabbed my purse, but I had to take care of a few things before leaving. I knew Stephen hated the smell of burned popcorn, so I went into both kitchens and microwaved two bags for five minutes each. As I reached the receptionist's area, Stacey was greeting Marcy, Stephen's wife. While they were talking, I walked by them very quickly. I didn't say good-bye. I pressed the "down" button for the elevator. As the doors opened, I placed a small box between them to hold it. I reopened the office doors, and Marcy was sitting nearby. She turned my way.

"Marcy, right?" I asked.

"Yes," she said with a smile.

"Stephen's gay."

Before she could answer, I was going down in the elevator, smiling as I inhaled the sweet smell of burned popcorn.

Several months later I heard that Stephen went to resign, and the company asked him to leave that minute. Joann was fired for stealing.

As I waited to cross the street on Seventh Avenue one very cold, brisk day, I turned to my right, and there was Stephen just staring at me.

I looked dead into his eyes. "Some protégé, huh, nitwit?" I said with a smile. I put my head up high and walked down 7th Avenue.

Seven

DONNY & CO.

Donny & Co. was a high-end men's and women's shoe line. The offices were on Fifty-Sixth Street and Seventh Avenue. There was a doorman in the lobby, and he had to call for approval to let anyone go up.

I interviewed with Ken Daniels for a traffic coordinator position.

There were three floors: on the forty-eighth was the showroom and sales office; on the thirty-fifth were accounts payable, order entry, and logistics; and on the fifteenth was Donny's office. The warehouse was in New Jersey.

Donny had been in business for more than fifteen years, selling high-end shoes. He was a hippie, always in jeans; a new crisp, white T-shirt; and turquoise accessories—rings, bracelets, and a matching belt.

Ken Daniels was the vice president only because he was good friends with Donny. He was about four feet, five inches tall, with bug eyes and a Napoleon complex. He didn't have a clue about the fashion or shoe business.

I was hired with a $3,500-a-year shoe allowance. The best part was the sample size was eight. Most companies' sample size was seven, never eight. I was lucky on that account. In fact I was in heaven. The shoes were expensive and beautiful.

The showroom was an oval-shaped space with plush rugs and a leather bench that curved around the windows. The shelves wrapped around the walls. It was just beautiful. What freaked me out was that when it got very windy outside, the building swayed from side to side. It kind of made me feel nauseous. And there was absolutely no eating in the showroom because Donny did not want the smell of food in there. It always smelled like lavender.

On my first day on the job, I met all of the staff. The office was filled with just women. Sigh. I took a long, deep breath and continued to meet the rest of the staff. I did the sign of the cross and said to myself, *Jesus Lord, help me.*

I would be on the thirty-fifth floor. There were five of us in the office and no manager. Everyone did her job, and if there were any issues we would talk to Ken, the vice president.

I got some supplies for my desk: pens, pencils, and paper clips, stuff like that. Nothing special. There was a corkboard on my wall for hanging papers. Everyone had the same one. After I put the supplies away, I turned and looked at everyone's desk and corkboard. Damn! They were filled with work-related stuff and lots of family pictures. My desk felt so lonely, and it was going to stay just like that. I didn't put any pictures on my board or any personal items on my desk. I didn't get comfortable anymore because I never knew—there was always someone around to mess things up. All I wanted to do if something happened was grab my coat and purse, and then I would be out.

Aida Gonzalez was a single, Spanish female who had been with the company for about five years. She was four foot three with frizzy hair. Her job was to import goods from Italy and Spain by working with customs brokers to clear shipments.

There were two open rooms. Amy, Sara, and Marie were in one room, and Aida and I were in the next. We were able to see each other from our desks.

Amy Turish was engaged to be married the next year. She was the bookkeeper and had been with the company for eight years. Amy and Sara were roommates.

Sara Hagan entered all of the orders. She'd been with the company for three years and was in the country on a work visa. Amy and Sara's grandparents were neighbors in Hungry. Sara was a very nice girl.

Marie Velez handled samples, sales reps' inquires, and customer service. She had been with the company for three years. Marie was married with two children and one on the way.

Aida and I sat with each other for a few days, going over the system and what she did at the company. We were both assigned to back each other up. She *seemed* nice, but I didn't trust her or anyone else anymore. I was on my own, like I had always been.

"Aida, do you have my pen?" I asked.

"Oh, yeah. Sorry. I always do that," she said.

As the orders and shipments came in and went out, things started to get really busy. Aida had been extremely busy.

"Aida, when you get a chance I need to know if the factory in Italy shipped the container for Saks Fifth Avenue," I said.

"Yeah, sure. I'll let you know in a bit," she said.

"OK."

"Give me half an hour."

"OK. Thanks."

An hour passed, and she never even looked my way, so I never asked again.

Aida told me they had shipped my container, but it had never left the factory. I have to do my own research because I was not getting a straight answer.

I walked over to Sara. "Yeah, Sara, do you have Batoli's e-mail address?"

"Sure. I'll send it to you," she said.

"Send me the contact person too. Thanks."

Batoli was one of our factories in Italy. Aida was in charge of it. I was not going to wait for her. I contacted them myself, and in minutes I got my shipping information. I had to e-mail someone six hours ahead and hundreds of miles away to get information I could have gotten from someone almost two feet in front of me.

Three days passed, and Aida never mentioned the information for which I had asked her. Maybe she forgot?

As I was waiting to go to the bathroom, Sara came out.

"Did you get the information you needed from Batoli?" she asked.

"Yes. Thanks. I'll come see you when I'm done," I said.

"OK."

After I left the bathroom, I walked over to Sara. On her desk was a vase of yellow and white roses.

"Wow, those flowers are beautiful!" I said.

"Aren't they? Donny gave them to me for my birthday."

"When was your birthday?" I asked.

"Friday," Sara said.

"Happy belated birthday."

"Thanks. He has a friend who owns a flower shop and he sends flowers to all the girls in the office for our birthdays."

"Nice. Oh, and thanks again. I spoke to Batoli, and they were able to help me."

"Waiting for Aida, you will never get anything," Sara said.

"Yup."

Damn. I needed answers when I needed them, not when Aida felt like giving them to me. I hoped she wasn't going to become a problem, but that wasn't anything I wasn't used to. Sigh.

Market Week (Spring/Summer)

During market week everyone worked the showroom, even on the weekends. Donny wanted all of us to wear black clothing. He also allowed us to pick out three pairs of the season's shoes to wear. It was good for the buyers to see the shoes. I liked going up to the showroom because of the lavender smell and all the beautiful flowers all around. I wanted to take them home with me.

After the last client left, Donny walked over to all of us.

"Hi, ladies," Donny said.

We all said hi.

"Thank you for all your help."

Everyone smiled and said, "You're welcome."

I was in the kitchen getting a cup of coffee when Donny walked in smiling.

"Hey, Anita, how's it going?" he asked.

"Good," I said with a smile. "And thanks for the shoes. They're awesome."

He looked at me googly-eyed.

"Here are some more." He pointed toward the shelves in the showroom, which had lots of shoes on them. He told me to take what I wanted, and I did. I wasn't greedy, but I got five pairs.

"Thank you, Donny," I said.

"Wear them with pleasure."

Everyone went back to work. As soon as I walked into the office, Aida asked, "What you got there?"

"Oh, these are shoes Donny gave me," I said.

"Really?"

"Yeah, really. You can ask him if you like."

"No, no. I was just asking," Aida said.

"And I'm just telling you." The last thing I needed was someone accusing me of stealing.

Dorothy was fixing Aida's computer. She turned around and said, "So, let's see them."

"Sure," I said. When I showed them the shoes, they looked at each other. "What?" I asked.

Aida said, "Nothing."

"Donny gave them to me."

"I know. He's like that."

I sat at my desk and continued to work. I didn't know what that was about. But whatever; I really didn't care.

Dorothy McGee was about five ten, with an arm full of tattoos; beautiful long, red, curly hair; and a nose ring. She was like a love child. She had been with the company for eight years. She handled all the IT issues.

Another market week (fall/holiday) approached, and I was just dying to get my hands on a few pairs of shoes I'd seen. We were all in the showroom, picking out our shoes and trying them on. It was great to get them for nothing.

Dorothy said, "Hey, look at these boots."

She had on black leather stiletto knee boots that looked hot on her because she was so tall. I'm not a lesbian, but if I think a woman looks hot, she gets my props.

"Wow, they look great on you!" I said.

Aida giggled like a high school girl, and everyone looked at her. She turned red and said, "Nice boots, Dorothy."

Amy said, "I want to get a pair too."

"Hey, guys, you know what I did this weekend?" Dorothy asked.

Aida jumped up. "What?"

"I got my nipples pierced."

"Ouch," I said.

Dorothy smiled and said, "Yeah."

Sara said, "Did it hurt?"

"No."

My nipples were hurting just thinking about Dorothy's.

"Can I see them?" Aida asked.

I turned red and didn't say anything. Everyone else giggled and waited for Dorothy's answer.

She gave us a big smile and said, "Sure!" Then she lifted her top and showed us her pieced nipples.

I couldn't believe she had done that. I immediately looked toward Aida. At first she turned as pale as a ghost; then she turned all red. She let out a weird giggle, like a hyena in heat.

I thought Aida secretly liked Dorothy. Maybe she had a crush on her. Maybe she was just excited because she was finally talking to the cool girls.

When I got back from lunch, there was no one in the office. My phone rang.

"Hello, this is Anita. How can I help you?"

"Hey, it's me, Sara. Come up to the showroom."

"OK." I found the call strange, but I went up anyway. It was kind of quiet as I turned the corner into the showroom.

Then everyone yelled, "Surprise! Happy birthday!"

I turned beet red. I was surprised they even knew it was my birthday. I'd never mentioned it to anyone. I guess they knew from my records.

They sang to me, and I blew out the candles on the chocolate truffle cake. It was delicious, and we all ate it. There is nothing better than a good piece of cake after lunch.

"Thank you, everyone," I said.

"You're welcome," they all said.

I helped Sara clean up and then headed back downstairs to my desk. "Sara, I'm going to use the bathroom. I'll meet you downstairs," I said.

"OK."

The other girls were already down there. When I opened the office door, all of them looked at me, smiling.

"What?" I asked.

Amy said, "Look," and pointed toward my desk.

We all looked and saw my red birthday roses.

"Wow, they are gorgeous," I said.

Sara, Amy, and Marie walked over to me.

Marie said, "You know, no one ever got red roses before."

"Really?" I asked.

"Marie's right," Sara said. "I've been here for eight years, and no one ever got red roses."

Amy said, "Uh, Donny loves you."

I laughed. "I don't think so."

Marie asked quietly, "Can you believe Dorothy showed us her pierced nipples?"

"I know, and did you see Aida's face?" Sara asked.

Marie said, "I think she has a crush on Dorothy."

"I'm sure she feels like she's finally a cool girl," I said.

We laughed so hard, but when Aida walked in we quickly stopped and went to our desks.

"What happened? What's so funny?" she asked.

Amy said, "Sara almost fell."

"Oh. That's not funny," Aida said and walked away.

We all giggled silently.

Christmas Party

The company's Christmas party was at the Four Seasons. There was a huge chandelier in the dining room. We all sat down at the table, and a waiter came around with menus. You know the food is very pricey when there are no prices on the menu.

Everyone ordered appetizers, drinks, and food. All of it was amazing. There were twenty-five of us. After the food and drinks, Donny gave out envelopes, and I was surprised to get one. I had been there for only six months. I didn't open it until I left the restaurant. I was surprised that my bonus was double my weekly salary. Merry Christmas to me.

As I walked toward the train station, I heard, "Hey, wait for me." I turned around. It was Aida.

"Are you walking to the train station?" I asked.

"Yes," she said.

"Are you going to Fifty-Seventh Street?"

"Yes."

"OK."

As we walked, we saw Ken pulling out of the garage in his Hummer.

"Wow, look at Ken's car," Aida said.

"That's a gas guzzler," I said.

"More like a substitution. You know—little man, big car? What is that phrase?"

"Napoleon complex," I said.

"Yeah, that's it. Napoleon complex." Aida giggled. She was a little tipsy. "Anita, what exactly does it mean?"

"It's when a short person, usually a man, feels inferior because of his size. He tends to take it out on people. He has anger issues, thrives on power, and buys big things—like a Hummer."

"Oh. That's probably why Ken's always mad."

—m—

I was swamped with orders and shipments. Donny was adding a handbag line, which meant more work for us all. I didn't mind. I loved being busy—it made the day go by faster.

I turned toward Aida and asked, "Aida, when is my February fifteenth shipment coming in?"

"I don't know. Let me check. I'll get back to you," she said.

"OK. Oh, and this is for you."

Aida turned around, and I gave her a gift. It was a pen I had made out of a fake sunflower plant.

"Is it real?" she asked.

I laughed. "No, silly, it's a pen." I pulled the sunflower out of the pot to show her the pen.

"Wow, thanks. This is great. Now I have my own pen," Aida said.

"Yeah, so you don't have to keep taking mine."

We both laughed.

"Thanks. I love it."

"You're welcome," I said.

Two weeks later I asked Aida for some information on a container, and again she pulled that shit about getting back to me. Another week passed. I had to say something.

"Aida, I need to know today, is my shipment coming or what?"

"What are you talking about?"

"I'm talking about the Bloomingdale's order I asked you about two weeks ago, and you never gave me any information."

"No, you didn't," she said.

"Oh yes, I did."

"Did not."

"Well, let me refresh your memory. You told me you would contact the broker again because of some issues you were having with him, but you were in a rush to go to lunch with Dorothy."

"Oh…yeah. Sorry," Aida said.

"Well, sorry is not going to help when Ken yells at me because the buyer is yelling at him. I need to know today! If you want I can check myself. Just give me the broker's e-mail address, and I'll copy you on everything I send."

"OK."

My phone rang. It was Ken asking about the Bloomingdale's order.

"What happened to the order, Anita? Where is it?"

"I should know soon. I asked Aida for the shipping information, and she told me she would let me know today."

"If we don't get it there by next week, the buyer will cancel the order."

"OK. I will keep you posted," I said.

"Thanks."

"Who was that?" Aida asked.

"That was Ken asking about the Bloomingdale's order."

"Oh, OK. I will send them an e-mail and copy you on it."

"Thanks," I said.

This bitch had better get me my information, or I was going to tell Ken. This had to come to an end.

Fifteen minutes later Aida said, "The Bloomingdale's order will be on time. I just got an e-mail from the broker that the container just left customs, and it's on the way to the warehouse."

"Great. Thanks for your help," I said.

I immediately called Ken. "Hi, Ken. It's Anita."

"Tell me good news."

"The container just left customs, and it's in route to the warehouse."

"Good job. Thanks."

I turned toward Aida and asked, "How long was the order stuck in customs?"

"About a week," she said.

"But I've been asking you about it for two weeks. You should have told me it was stuck in customs last week."

"Well, you know now."

I stared at her for a second. "Well, I could have known a week ago."

"Next time then," Aida said.

"Listen, I'm not here to argue with you. I'm here to do a job, so please lose the attitude. A few weeks ago, I asked you about Batoli for Saks Fifth Avenue, and you never answered me."

"I did answer you," Aida said.

"No, you didn't. I e-mailed Batoli myself and got the information from them."

"You're not allowed to e-mail them," she said.

I started laughing. "Says who?"

She stayed quiet because she knew she was wrong, and Sara, Marie, and Amy were all listening to our argument. What a nitwit.

———※———

Two weeks later Ken called me into his office. "Please sit," he said. I sat with my game face on. I knew what was about to happen. I had been there before.

"Anita, the company has come to a decision. We decided this is not going to work. We are relieving you of your duties."

"OK," I said.

He looked like he had seen a ghost. He was stunned because all I said was OK.

"Oh, and I don't have a complex," Ken said.

"What?" I asked.

"Aida told me what you said about me."

"Really? Is that the reason you're letting me go? To be honest with you, she was the one who mentioned it. Anyway, you think about that." I didn't give him a chance to answer me. I walked out of his office.

I didn't say a word to the girls. I just grabbed my coat and purse, and I walked out.

—⚶—

In order to go up to the office, the doorman in the lobby had to call for someone to approve it. The next day I sent my cousin Sandy, to the office building, and she told the doorman she needed to speak to Aida at Donny & Co.

"Aida, there's someone who needs to speak to you. Hold on," he said.

He handed Sandy the phone.

"Bring down the flower pen Anita made for you, and leave it in the lobby," Sandy said.

"Uh, sure."

Sandy gave the phone back to the doorman. "Thanks. She's coming down. I'll be back."

"OK."

Ten minutes later, when Sandy returned, the flower pen was in the lobby. The doorman gave it to her.

"Thank you," Sandy said.

—⚶—

While looking for another job I was also busy making my handbags and selling them to small boutiques. The money was OK, but I needed a job.

Eight

Essex

After several months of job searching, I was hired at Essex to handle their shipping, invoicing, and order entry. I work the red jacket with black pencil pants and Tory Burch ballet flats. Essex was well known for aviator leather jackets. The company had been in business for more than forty years. Ira, the owner, had purchased a license to design apparel—jeans and T-shirts for junior girls.

Ira Grossman had been in the denim business for twenty-five years. He bragged about it all the time. I think he had Tourette syndrome because he twitched his head, neck, and shoulders. He cursed all day at someone in the office or over the phone. He was stuck in the '70s, with his open button-down shirts with gold chain.

It was a small office. When you walked in, you were in the showroom. Behind the wall were three desks where Rosy, Frank, and Richie sat, and then Ira's small office was behind them. I was stationed in the showroom because there wasn't a desk available for me yet.

Two months later we moved to another building with so much more space for everyone. The showroom had enough room for the sales reps to show the line. It was just in time for market week. And to my surprise, my desk was at the front. I was the receptionist. Ira should have told me. I don't like liars, and I was pissed, but I got over it because I didn't want to keep jumping from job to job.

It was one of those Monday mornings when everything that could go wrong went wrong. It was pouring rain outside; I got splashed by a car; the trains were delayed; and I forgot my lunch.

When I got to the office, Ira was the only one there. He had a camera outside the glass doors that led into the office, to watch who was coming in and going out.

He unlocked the door. "What happened to you?" he asked.

I sighed and walked into the office. "The trains were delayed. I guess everyone is having the same problem, huh?"

"I didn't have a problem."

"I wouldn't have a problem either if I lived in the city," I said.

He smirked, and I walked away. Everyone started coming in shortly after that.

There was a sensor on the door, and every time someone walked into the office an annoying bell rang: ding-dong. It served its purpose because I knew when someone was walking in.

Richie Pellegrino was the in-house sales rep. He was a short Italian guy who reminded me of Joe Pesci. He and Ira had worked together in another company. He'd been with the company for two years.

Richie walked in while I was busy entering some orders. I didn't hear him come in.

"Good morning, Anita."

I looked up. "Hey. Good morning, Richie."

"What happened to the ding-dong?"

I pointed to Ira's office. "He's in his office."

We both laughed.

"The trains were bad. Did you have any problems coming in?" Richie asked.

"I sure did."

"What a way to start off a Monday."

"It could always be worse," I said.

"Sure could." Richie said.

Rosy was a retired bookkeeper who came in once a week to help Ira. She wore pink lipstick and a big, red wig. Every time she scratched her head, the wig moved back and forth. And she was constantly clearing her throat. It sounded like she had been smoking for years. She was a nice lady and funny too.

When Ira had nothing to do, he walked around the office to see what everyone else was doing. Once he walked over to Rosy, who asked him about some accounting issues while scratching her wig back and forth and clearing her throat. Then he turned to me.

"Yo, Anita. What you doing?"

"I'm doing what you're paying me to do: my job."

"Yeah?" He laughed and then walked back to his office.

Chloe came in once a week to discuss styles and what the urban market was doing, but her designs were awful. It looked like a second grader sketched them. But she talked a good game. She was freelancing for at least two other companies.

Chloe was showing Ira some samples she'd bought from several stores that represented what was happening in the urban market. Ira called everyone into the showroom to see them.

"Anita, what do you think?" he asked.

"I like the fabric, and the colors are nice," I said.

Frank walked over and touched the fabric. "Nice for the urban market. Like that guy, Huffy. The creator of hip-hop."

"Who?" Chloe asked.

"You know, that guy, Huffy."

I said, "Frank, Huffy is a bike. You mean the rapper, Puffy. Sean 'Diddy' Combs. He was not the one who created hip-hop."

Everyone laughed.

Frank was old school. He'd been in the business for more than forty years. He was about seventy-five years old. He and Ira also went way back. They had been in business together years ago.

Frank didn't want to stay home because he was bored, and he liked to stay busy. He also liked to ruffle some feathers in the office, he said, like in the olden days. He made all the cash on delivery (COD) calls to the customers. It made him feel important. He really was important because our weekly paychecks depended on those calls. He was always in the office very early to start his day. He walked very slowly and took his time.

Ira was always yelling and cursing at someone over the phone or in the office. I always tried to stay under the radar, but because the office was not big, it was impossible. I was ready for him because I was not going to take his verbal abuse. I think he knew that but might test the waters.

While the spring and summer lines were starting to ship, things got very busy for those of us entering orders and invoicing. Everyone was running around, getting the fall line ready for the showroom. Ira hired two people that week: Laura a designer and Tommy a production manager. Laura was very gothic and always looked very tired. She was pale, with dark circles around her eyes. Her hair was jet black, and she always wore black.

Tommy was Chinese and a very nice man. Even though his English was not great, he worked very hard.

While I was washing my hands in the ladies room, Laura walked in.

"Hi, Anita. How's it going?" she asked.

"It's going," I said. I really wanted to tell her the truth that Ira was a lunatic. But I couldn't. She would have to see for herself.

—◆—

Ira yelled, "What the fuck happened?"

He walked into his office with Frank and then slammed the door. All we could hear was Ira yelling and cursing. Frank was in charge of sending the factor invoices. The factor was our bank. We let them know the invoices we had, and they sent us an amount for working capital.

Ira had given Frank an amount he needed for that week, but Frank had given the bank the wrong amount. Ira had been lying to the factor about how much money was coming in.

He walked out of his office. "Hello, everyone. Please meet me in the showroom."

After everyone sat down, he said, "OK, guys. We need to start selling more goods—especially COD! Get on the phone, and start making calls. The meeting is over. Thank you."

———✲———

While I was helping Rosy with a spreadsheet, I turned back around to my desk and saw Laura taking a sip of my coffee.

My eyes opened wide. "What the fuck are you doing?"

She put my coffee down and smiled. "I just wanted a sip."

"Don't ever do that again," I said. "Here, take the rest of it."

"No, I'm going down to get Starbucks."

"Well, get me a large cappuccino, and it's on you."

Laura smiled and said, "OK."

The phone rang. It was Russell calling for Ira.

"Ira, Russell is on line one," I said.

"Tell him I'm on the phone."

"Russell," I said after I switched lines, "Ira's on the phone. He'll call you back."

"OK. I'll call him again," Russell said.

I went to the back to fax some orders to the warehouse. Richie was also faxing.

"Where's Laura?" he asked.

"Getting me coffee. Why?"

"You're not going to believe what she did," he said.

"Try me, because you're not going to believe what she did to me. You first."

"I was on a sales call, and I had a cup of coffee and a muffin. I like to separate the top of the muffin from the bottom, so I can eat it last. Laura came out of nowhere and broke the top of the muffin in half and started eating it. The top of my muffin! That's the best part. Can you believe that?"

"Oh my God. Yeah, I can believe it because she was downing your muffin with my coffee," I said.

"What do you mean?"

"She took a sip of my coffee behind my back while I was working with Rosy!"

"Oh my God. No, she didn't."

"Yes, she did. She's not all there," I said.

While I was walking back to my desk, Laura walked into the office.

"Sorry about that," she said as she handed me my coffee.

"Thanks," I said.

She walked away. Then I turned to Richie and said, "You should have told her to get you a muffin."

"I know; I should have. She's got a lot of nerve."

"She's really ballsy," I said.

When I returned to my desk, the phone rang.

"Ira, Russell's on line three," I said.

"Tell him I'm out to lunch," Ira said.

"OK."

The T-shirt samples were coming in, and Ira was in a good mood until he opened the box. Then we heard him yelling at Tommy.

"What the fuck happened? They were supposed to ship yesterday, and now you're telling me they won't ship until next month?"

"We have to wait until they finish with the quota," Tommy said.

Tommy was trying to explain to Ira that the factories were shipping the T-shirts late due to some kind of quota in China. Ira didn't want to hear it. Tommy didn't deserve to be spoken to like that.

"I can't fucking believe this. OK, just keep me posted." Ira got up and walked away.

Every time a new T-shirt came in, I was the fit model. The office was so cold that my nipples would be out in full effect. I would breathe hot air on them, but it didn't work. I usually had to try on five to ten T-shirts. The fittings would last about twenty minutes. I got smart and started wearing a padded bra, and then the fittings only lasted ten minutes.

TGIF (thank God it's Friday). It was payday. Ira had his door closed all day and asked me to take messages. At 5:00 p.m. I wanted to get my check. Forget about direct deposit—that was another issue. If Ira did direct deposit our paychecks, the money would automatically come out of his bank account, and he wanted to hold on to his money for as long as he could. So we got company checks, and by the time he decided to give them out, the banks were already closed.

I knocked on Ira's door.

"Yeah!" he yelled.

I opened the door.

He looked up over his eyeglasses. "What?"

"I'm leaving, and I need my check," I said.

He smiled and handed it to me. "Don't cash it until Tuesday."

"Tuesday? You've got to be kidding me. What am I supposed to do for the weekend? Starve? I'm going to cash it downstairs at the cashier."

"Yeah, that's a good idea. Do that," Ira said.

I pointed my finger at him and said, "It better not bounce." Then I walked out.

After waiting twenty minutes on line at the check-cashing place, I finally got to the cashier.

She looked at the check and said, "I can't cash this."

"Why?"

"Because that company's checks have bounced."

"Damn!"

I was so embarrassed and pissed that I called Ira at the office, but there was no answer. He must have left. As I was leaving the check-cashing place, I ran into him.

"Ira! These people are saying your checks are bouncing, and they're not going to cash my check, so you need to give me at least one hundred dollars."

He started twitching. "Those people have it in for me. I don't know what they're talking about."

He pulled a bundle of money out of his pocket and gave me a hundred-dollar bill. I immediately scratched Benjamin's face for the ridges and then held it up to the light to make sure I saw the serial numbers.

"It's real," Ira said.

"You never know. Here, take it back. Give me twenties instead."

"It's real."

"I know, but I prefer twenties," I said. "And from now on, I want cash or direct deposit. I'm not going through this shit again."

I never gave him a chance to respond. I walked away. Damn nitwit.

I knew I would not be there for much longer based on how things were going. Ira had not cursed me out yet, but I knew it was coming, and I was ready for him.

—⚏—

The following Friday Ira handed me an envelope. In it was a real paycheck, not a company check. And it was only noon.

"Thanks, Ira," I said.

"Sure. No problem."

The phone rang. I answered it.

"Ira, Russell is one line three," I said. "He says he needs to talk to you about the money you owe him."

"Tell him I'm not here," Ira said.

"OK."

When I was getting ready to leave, a black couple walked into the office.

"Hi, we're here to see Ira," the man said.

"Sure. Your name?" I asked.

"Tell him Kevin and the model are here."

"Sure." I called Ira and told him they were there to see him.

"You can have a seat in the showroom. He'll be with you shortly," I said.

Model? I didn't know Ira was looking for a model. Five minutes later I walked into his office. "Ira, Kevin and the model are here."

"Oh, yeah, I'll be right out. Have a good weekend."

"Yeah, you too. Also, you know Russell has been calling you? He said he needs to talk to you."

"Yeah, I know. I'll talk to him when I'm ready."

"OK."

I walked out of his office and didn't think anything of it, but I had to return to the office because I had forgotten my shopping bag. I had to knock on the glass door because it was locked. Ira was surprised and opened the door.

"What happened?" He was standing in front of the door.

"I forgot my shopping bag. Are you going to let me in?"

He was nervous. "Sure," he said.

I looked into the showroom, and there were two black girls wearing the new T-shirt line. There were several Polaroid pictures on the table. I thought Ira was up to no good. He probably told them he wanted to use them for advertising. He was probably going to take the pictures home and do you know what. Yuck.

—◊◊—

Ira always strolled around the office like a tough guy.

"Hey, Tommy, where are the goods? Are you stupid or what? Get them here. I need to ship them. Do I have to tell you in Chinese?"

"They already shipped, Ira!"

I smiled at Tommy and gave him a thumbs-up. I was happy for him because he kind of yelled back. I felt bad for him because he worked hard, and Ira was abusive. I just wanted to punch Ira in the mouth.

"Ira, Russell is on line two again," I said.

"Tell him I'm out."

"Russell, he stepped out."

"Yeah, I'm sure he did," Russell said, and then the phone went dead.

A few seconds later, Ira walked over to me. "I have a dentist appointment," he said. "I'll be back later."

It was strange that he seemed nervous, and he was leaving via the freight elevator instead of the regular elevator. He knew Russell was looking for him.

The phone rang again. It was Russell.

"Let me speak to Ira now!"

"He stepped out of the office. Who's calling?" I asked.

"It's Russell. Tell that motherfucker I'm coming to the office." He hung up the phone.

I ran to the back. "Hey, guys, does anyone know who Russell is?"

Frank turned his chair around and said, "Russell produces some of our jeans, and Ira owes him a lot of money."

"Well, he's coming here to look for Ira."

Twenty minutes later I heard the bell. I looked up, and it was Russell.

"Hi, Anita. Is that fucking prick in?"

"No."

"Yeah, where is he?" he asked.

"He went to the dentist, but he'll be back."

"I'm going to wait."

"OK. You can sit in the showroom," I said.

I turned around, and Rosy's eyes were wide open, like a deer in headlights.

"Oh my God, Anita," she said in a whisper. "He's going to wait?"

"Yup," I said.

"What are we going to do?" she asked.

"Nothing, What can we do?"

Russell waited in the showroom for an hour. There was no sign of Ira. Finally Russell came back out.

"I'll be back," he said. "Tell that twitching motherfucker that I'll be back."

As soon as he left, Ira snuck in like nothing was happening. He smiled and said, "Hey, what's going on? Anyone looking for me?"

"What's going on?" Rosy asked. "Ira! Russell was here looking for you."

"OK," Ira said. He rushed into his office, and ten minutes later he came out with his briefcase. "I'm leaving for the day. See you tomorrow."

"Russell's coming back," I said.

He just waved his hands in the air as if to say, "Whatever." Ira usually walked around like a tough guy. On that day he was running like a punk.

An hour later I heard the ding-dong and looked up. Russell walked in yelling, "Ira, you motherfucker. Where's my money?"

He went straight to Ira's office, thinking he would be there, and when he didn't find him Russell ransacked Ira's office. Everyone left, went to the lobby, and told security what was happening. Security called the police. We didn't know what Russell was capable of.

While we waited for the police, Laura was outside, deeply inhaling a cigarette. Frank and Rosy talked about Russell while Rosy scratched her wig back and forth and cleared her throat. Chloe walked over to us.

"Hey, guys, what's going on? Why are you all down here?" she asked.

"Some crazy man is looking for Ira," I said. "He owes the guy money. The man was ransacking Ira's office, so we all came down here."

"Wow, that's crazy. I was coming here for a check."

"I don't think that will happen today," I said.

"Yeah I see that. Damn."

"Do you know anyone who's hiring? I'm not staying with this company long," I said.

"As a matter of fact, I do. I freelance for this company called Willows. The contact's name is Krisann. Here's her number," Chloe said.

"Thanks, Chloe."

The police went upstairs while we all stayed in the lobby. Twenty minutes later an officer came down and said, "It's a mess, but you can go up now."

When we walked into the office, everything seemed OK except for Ira's office. His computer was smashed on the floor. The glass shelves were also smashed, and glass was all over the place.

Ira walked in. "Is everyone OK?" He was twitching almost every few words. He was nervous.

We all said yes.

"There's no damage here," he said. "What are the police talking about?"

We all looked at each other. Rosy cleared her throat, scratched her wig, and then said, "Not your office."

Ira twitched repeatedly. It was hard for him to talk, so he just walked to his office. That was karma for him because he was such a nice man. Hmm.

After the police left, everyone helped clean the office and then we all went home for the day.

The next morning Ira gave me a check for Russell. It was for what he owed him: $10,000. That was a lot of money. I would be pissed too, but now Ira was going to sue Russell for the damages—probably for the $10,000 he owed Russell.

—⁙—

It was my turn for Ira to yell at me.

"Anita. What the fuck happened to that account?"

"What fucking account?" I asked.

"You know which account. The one you fucked up," he said.

"I didn't fuck up any account. Now, what are you talking about?"

"You were supposed to ship COD, and now it's on credit with the factor."

"Yeah, the report says it's on the factor's list. Here." I threw the report on his desk. "And let me tell you something, you have two daughters. Would you want someone to talk to them the way you're talking to me? Watch yourself. Here are your keys. I'm giving you two weeks' notice." I walked away.

Ira was upset that I was leaving. Frank tried to convince me to stay. "Are you still leaving?" he asked.

"Yes, Frank, I'm leaving—next week, not in two weeks. You can tell him that."

I gave my notice without having another job. I'd just had it with the yelling and the cursing and the people coming there and breaking stuff. On top of all of that, the paychecks were not reliable.

I called Krisann at Willows and met with her during my lunch break. At first I was nervous without my interview suit, but she hired me on the spot. I gave Ira one week and then I was off to Willows. Six months later Ira lost the license to sell Essex because he broke the contract rules.

It felt good not to get fired. That time it was my choice.

Nine

WILLOWS

Willows was a women's apparel line with some sports inspiration. It was sweat suits, denim pants and jackets, and some dresses.

The office was on Thirty-Third Street and Broadway, on the twelfth floor. There were only three tenants on the floor, and every office had its own bathroom down the hall.

I rang the bell. The door was made of glass, so I could see Krisann coming to open the door. Oh my God. She looked like a tomato had exploded on her. She was dressed in a red from head to toe. Her suit, blouse, shoes, and even her stockings were red. And she wanted to design clothing. Scary.

Krisann Willows had grown up competing in pageants. She'd won Lil Miss Dallas, Miss Junior Dallas, and Miss Texas. She had been a runner-up for Miss USA. She had her whole office decorated with her pageant pictures from five years old on. All she talked about was her pageants. She was the mother of twin high school boys, and she was married to a major league baseball player. Krisann was an only child. She had everything and anything she wanted.

"Good morning, Anita," she said.

"Good morning. How are you?" I asked.

"Fine. Welcome to Willows."

"Thank you." Oh boy. I hoped the job would work out, at least for a while. I was tired of moving around.

The office had three offices, two small ones and one large. The large office was Krisann's. She displayed all her pageant trophies on a dusty, glass wall unit.

The showroom was very plain. The white walls needed new paint. There was a table with five chairs and grids on the wall to hang the line. There was a stockroom packed with merchandise, a small refrigerator, a microwave, a coffee machine, and a copy machine.

"This is your office," she told me, showing me into it. "You will be sharing it with Brandy." There were two small desks facing each other and one computer.

"Brandy and Keisha are part-time employees. They both go to school" Krisann said.

Brandy and Keisha both attended FIT. They were nice young ladies.

"When are they here?" I asked.

"Brandy comes in every day except Thursday, and Keisha comes in three days a week: Monday, Wednesday, and Thursday."

"Oh, good. I'll get to meet them both today."

"Yes, you will. Over here is the middle office for our sales rep, if we ever find one," Krisann said.

That sure didn't sound good. She had been in business for three years. Sigh.

Later we were in my office going over the computer system and filling out paperwork for payroll. I heard the door open, and Brandy and Keisha both walked in.

"Good morning, ladies," Krisann said.

They both said, "Good morning."

"This is Anita. She's our new traffic coordinator."

"Hi, Anita," they said. I shook both of their hands.

"Brandy, Anita will be sitting at the desk with the computer," Krisann said.

"OK," Brandy said.

When I was done with the paperwork, Brandy and Keisha showed me everything in the stockroom. Someone rang the doorbell. Keisha opened the door. It was Chloe.

"Hi, Chloe," Keisha said.

"Hi, ladies. Anita, you're here."

"Yes, I'm here. Thanks again," I said. We hugged.

"You're welcome. How are you?"

"Good." I said.

"Is Krisann here?"

Brandy said, "I'll let her know you're here."

Chloe had come to show Krisann her sketches and samples for the new spring line. They sat in the showroom. The door bell rang again, and it was Donald.

"Krisann, I have Bank of America on the phone for you." I said.

"Sure. I'll take it in my office," she said.

"OK. Line two."

"Chloe, I'll be right back. Work with Donald," Krisann said.

"OK," Chloe said.

Donald was a production manager for another company. He had been in the business for more than thirty years. He helped Krisann with the production and connected her with factories she could work with overseas.

Krisann needed more sales and finally hired a rep, Sam Jones, to sell her line. She was going to Chicago for the day to meet with Sam and take him the line. According to Krisann he had his own office, and he was representing other lines.

For the first couple of months, Sam was sending a handful of orders every couple of days. Krisann was getting excited and started ordering more quantities from the factory. We were shipping every day, but it wasn't enough. She was hoping for larger orders.

Then the orders stopped, and Krisann was not happy at all.

"Any new orders come in today?" She would ask this every day.

"No, not yet," I replied. "Ever think about selling your inventory to closeouts?"

She looked at me like I'd insulted her. "No!"

"Why not? We have a lot of inventory we can sell."

"But not to discounters. Plus I'm doing an event soon, and we can sell stuff there," she said.

"OK."

Krisann needed to get rid of her inventory. No one was going to keep buying the same line year after year. After several weeks she stopped asking if we'd received any orders. I turned to Brandy and Keisha. "Can you guys help me count the inventory in the stockroom?"

"Sure," said Brandy.

"When?" Keisha asked.

"Can we start today?"

They both said yes.

Krisann walked out of her office. "Hey, guys, what do you think about having a Thanksgiving lunch in the showroom?"

"Sure. What's on the menu?" Keisha said.

"Everyone can bring a dish—store bought or homemade."

"Sure, I can bring *arroz con gandules* and *penil*," I said.

Keisha asked, "What is that?"

"Rice with pigeon peas and roast pork."

"I love Spanish food. I can bring some corn bread."

Brandy said, "Me too. I can bring some collard greens and sweet-potato pie."

"Great," Krisann said. "My mom is making mac and cheese and some other stuff, and I'll bring the drinks. Sam Jones, the rep from Chicago, will be joining us. He is bringing the plates and utensils."

I made sure the table in the showroom was cleaned with Clorox wipes, the rug was vacuumed daily if needed, and the bathroom was cleaned. Mrs. Wright was coming to town, so Krisann made sure her office was spotless, otherwise that shit was a mess. The closet in her office was piled knee-high with dirty clothes.

The bathroom was another story. Krisann was a pig. She never cleaned it, nor did she ever look to see if she'd left anything behind. So, of course, I had to keep it clean. She should have made an effort.

Mrs. Wright was Krisann's mom. She visited New York every few months and stayed for the holidays. She lived in Dallas with her husband (Krisann's dad), but she always came to New York alone.

Everyone was there for lunch: Brandy, Keisha, Chloe, Mrs. Wright, Sam Jones, Krisann, and I. Sam brought the brought paper plates, cups, and plastic forks and knives.

We said grace and chowed down. The food was great. After lunch we all cleaned up and continued with the workday.

"Anita, can you invoice this order for Sam?" Krisann asked.

"Sure, where is he?"

"He's in the bathroom."

"OK," I said.

Krisann and Sam were in the stockroom picking out his order when I gave him the invoice. I noticed he had a shopping bag with the plates, forks, and knives he had brought with him. I just looked at him, thinking, *Damn, you're taking them back.* It was bad enough that he'd peed all over the damn toilet seat. If he couldn't pee standing up then he should have sat down. And at least he should have cleaned up after himself. I wanted to tell him that so badly, but I didn't. The worst part was that I had to clean it because no one else at the office cleaned the bathroom even though we all had to use it. That was bullshit. I hadn't signed up for that.

When Sam left I said to everyone, "I can't find the plates."

Krisann said, "But they were just here."

Keisha said, "Let me check the stockroom."

"Don't bother. I think Sam took them back," I said.

Brandy said, "No, he didn't."

"Then where are the plates, knives, and forks?" I asked.

Mrs. Wright said, "That is so damn ghetto."
We all laughed.

———∞———

Krisann was trying to keep her business open. Her husband was a silent partner, and he wanted to stay that way. He occasionally attended meetings in the office, but he really did it to only make Krisann happy.

Earl Willows was Krisann's husband. He used to play professional baseball for the New York Mets. After he'd stopped playing, he'd started running several businesses from his home office. Krisann used his fame to get her line out there. The line was not good enough to stand alone; she needed a better designer and more money.

We were preparing for our Christmas event. Krisann was going to preview her spring collection, which Chloe had designed. Krisann booked a few people to come and sell their own merchandise. She was charging twenty dollars at the door, food and drinks included.

One company that came to sell its merchandise was called Touch and Go. They sold spa stuff, like candles, soaps, lotion, and towels. They were set up in my office. The middle office was for Made in the Shade. They sold all kinds of makeup for all types of skin colors.

In Krisann's office the inventory was displayed on racks and models. In the showroom was the catered food. There were two tables filled with fried chicken, mac and cheese, desserts, and lots of other food from a place called Harlem's Soul Food. It was good—especially the cupcakes.

There was another table in the hallway for people to pay and to check their coats. There was a good turn out; we sold merchandise. Krisann looked happy, so I knew she'd made some money. I was happy for her because that meant we all would be getting paid the following week.

Things went pretty good for that first year. I was getting weekly checks. We held several fashion shows events in churches, night clubs, and the showroom. The line was selling, but it still was not enough. Krisann hired a sales rep from a fashion show she'd held in a night club, as the Chicago rep was not sending any more orders. We would see how things worked out.

Every morning when I walked into the office at nine o'clock, the phone rang. It was always Krisann, making sure I had arrived on time. She would make up something to say, but she was really calling to check up on me. She could check up on me anytime she liked because I always arrived on time unless there was train trouble.

"Good morning. Willows," I said.

"Good morning, Anita."

"Good morning, Krisann."

"Oh, by the way, I hired a new sales rep, and he'll be there this afternoon. I should be there in a few minutes. I need help with some boxes, so please come down to help me."

"Sure." I looked at Brandy as I hung up.

"What happened?" she asked.

"We have to go down and help Krisann with some boxes."

"Oh, damn!"

I laughed. "I know, but when she calls we go."

An hour later Krisann called the office. "Hi, Brandy. Please come down and help me with these boxes."

"OK." Brandy hung up and said to me, "Let's go. She's in the parking lot."

"Let's bring the cart," I said.

"Oh, yeah, good idea."

Brandy and I went down to help Krisann. She'd parked her car and had several boxes on the sidewalk for us to take upstairs.

"Can you guys please put these in the showroom, so we can sort out the inventory?" Krisann asked.

We said OK and looked at each other.

"Damn, these boxes are heavy," I said.

"Thank God we have this cart," Brandy said.

"I know, because they would break my back."

We were happy to see Keisha walking toward us. She helped us with the six boxes. Brandy and I were then counted inventory and put it in the stockroom for Magic and the Fashion Ski Show in Pittsburgh.

"Between us, Krisann cannot keep a sales rep," Brandy said.

"Why?" I asked.

"She doesn't want to pay."

"Does she pay you?"

"Yeah, and she pays Keisha too."

"Good."

Keisha walked into the stockroom and said, "She sometimes makes us wait a week or two for our paychecks."

"Ah, damn! Really?" I said.

"Shh. You never heard that from us" Brandy said.

"No, of course not. I would never say you said it. I'm sure she'll do it to me too." I sighed deeply. None of that sounded good. "I need to talk to her about getting our checks direct deposited."

"I don't have a bank account, so that will not work for me," Brandy said.

"Neither do I," said Keisha.

"I'll talk to her. I just came from a company that did the same shit to me. I'm not going to do this anymore. Also you guys should have bank accounts. It's good to have one."

Krisann arrived with the new part-time sales rep. "Good morning, everyone. This is our new house sales rep, Collin."

We all said hi.

"Collin will be in the office once or twice a week. The rest of the week, he will be on the road." She turned to him. "Please fax all the orders to Anita, and she'll process them and ship them depending on credit approvals."

Collin had been in New York for a while. He'd left his wife and two children in California. He was selling the line, and it was hard because most buyers had never heard of Willows. Of course we all had to throw in that Krisann was married to Earl Willows from the Mets. Believe it or not, it helped even though the line was not strong.

That year Krisann decided she wanted to go to Magic, an apparel show held in Las Vegas twice a year, in February and August. Anyone and everyone showed their clothing lines at Magic. It was one of the biggest apparel shows.

We were preparing for the February show: getting samples, videos, TVs, lights, order forms, and so on. As the day was getting closer, we were not sure if there would be enough money for all of us to go. Four of us were going: Krisann, her mother, Collin, and I. Krisann were trying to get the hotel rooms for nothing because of who her husband was.

Everything had to be shipped to Las Vegas before we arrived at the hotel. Of course there were several items shipped at the last minute.

Las Vegas

We arrived on a Sunday afternoon, and it was very cold. I was prepared with a coat, a hat, and gloves. Krisann and her mother flew first class, while Collin and I flew coach. We sat together for five hours. He was cool and so ghetto.

When we arrived Krisann wanted to go straight to the convention center, to make sure all of the boxes were there. Everything was there. As she took the line out of the boxes, she discovered that everything was wrinkled.

She said, "We need a steamer badly."

"What happened?" I asked.

"Look at the line. It's all wrinkled. We need to steam everything."

"Maybe the hotel has one."

"Where are you going?" Krisann asked.

I said, "I'll be back." I went around the convention center, and hit the jackpot. I found a steamer and brought it over to our booth. Krisann and Collin were looking at me strangely, but they were smiling.

"OK. We can start steaming the line," I said.

"Oh my God, where did you get that?" Krisann asked.

"Shh. I borrowed it from another booth. So let's chop-chop and get it done, so I can put it back."

Krisann giggled and said, "Oh, great because we can't sell wrinkled clothes."

"Damn girl, you're good," Collin said.

"Collin, go get some water so we can pour it in here," Krisann said.

"I already put water in it," I said.

"From where?" Colin asked.

"I had a bottle of water in my bag." I said

—⟋⟍—

After three hours of trying to get stuff done at the booth, we all went to dinner. I was so exhausted. All I wanted to do was sleep. We hit the buffet at the hotel's restaurant.

While eating dinner Krisann said, "I'm sure we're all exhausted. Let's all meet in the morning for breakfast before heading to the convention center."

Mrs. Wright said, "Yes, child. Mama is tired. And you know I love my slot machines, but I ain't even looking that way."

Collin said, "Mrs. Wright, you are really funny."

"Do you gamble, Anita?" Mrs. Wright asked.

"No, I don't."

"Good. And you, Collin?"

"No, ma'am, I don't gamble either," Collin said.

"OK. Let's meet around seven," said Krisann. "We'll have breakfast and still have enough time to head to the convention center. It opens at eight for the vendors and to the public at ten. That's enough time to get everything ready."

I said quickly, "OK. See you in the morning."

Everyone called it a night. There was a lot to do the next day. The first day was always the busiest and the hardest. I showered and went straight to sleep. I made sure to get a wake-up call because I knew I wouldn't get up on time on my own.

Monday

I felt like I'd never gone to sleep because I was so exhausted. At seven I was the first one in the lobby. Five minutes later Collin, Krisann, and Mrs. Wright appeared. Everyone said good morning to each other, and we headed to the restaurant. Everything was buffet style and all you can eat every day, all day. When I looked around at the buffet area (all you can eat), I noticed there were a lot of oversized people. I thought people really went to Las Vegas just for the buffet.

The table was silent as we all stuffed our faces with food. I was so full, I couldn't move.

"Is everyone ready? We have a long day and week ahead of us," Krisann asked.

I said, "Yes, I'm ready."

With a toothpick in his mouth, Collin rubbed his stomach and said, "I'm as ready as I'll ever be."

"By the way, I'm giving the person who sells the most fifteen hundred dollars," Krisann said.

I wasn't really sure why I was there because back in New York, I ran the office and shipped the merchandise. I did not do sales. But for $1,500, I could surely try.

Collin looked at me. "Ready to lose, Brooklyn?"

I smiled and said, "Bring it, Cali."

We took a cab to the convention center. It was about a ten-minute ride from the hotel. It was very cold our. My body ached, but I thought it was just from being tired from the flight and working late at the booth. I took two aspirins and drank some orange juice, hoping the pain would go away. I was also hoping to make some money and get rid of the awful inventory.

It wasn't going to be easy to sell the line, especially when no one knew about it. People think they can just design a clothing line and sell it. It takes a lot more than that. It takes a lot of money too.

The line had two sweat suits—one in cotton and the other in nylon. The cotton sweat suits would shrink by 18 percent when washed, and Krisann knew that all long. But she told us to sell them, and we had a lot of them. The denim items in the line included two jackets, one bolero, a three-quarter-length jacket, a pair of jeans. There were also T-shirts and several nylon dresses in different lengths and colors.

People started entering the convention center. At one point it got really crowded, but not everyone was looking our way. They had never heard of the line, so they didn't bother to look. We were all just sitting there waiting for customers to check out the line.

I said to Krisann and Collin, "I will be back."

I took a bunch of our cards and flyers and handed them out to the people passing by. Before I knew it, we were busy selling the line. People were coming to see me. I thought it was my leather pants and my cropped tee that brought customers to the booth. I was selling the line and working the show. It was a lot of work. I was there all day, walking around and talking to people.

Collin said to me, "Yo, how did you get these people over here?

"You nitwit. I gave them flyers. Plus the outfit helped," I said.

"Damn. I didn't know we had flyers."

"Next time do your homework."

There were so many vendors with outrageous booths. It took a lot of money to do that. Krisann could not afford it. We had the line and a fashion show video.

That night we all went out to dinner. All I wanted to do was go to bed. My throat was hurting, and I felt ill. We all walked into the lobby of the hotel and headed to the buffet.

I said, "I'm going to use the bathroom. I'll meet you back here."

"OK," Krisann said.

The woman on line in front of me to go into the ladies' room had her period. I could smell it, and it made me feel nauseous. The air was so dry, I was able to smell everything.

When I got to the table with my food, I sat next to Mrs. Wright. The stench of ass crossed my nose. *Damn!* My stomach turned, and my eyes watered. It was all over. I turned toward Mrs. Wright.

"What's wrong, baby?" she asked. She saw the look on my face.

"I'm not feeling well," I said.

Krisann looked at me. "Are you OK?"

"No. I'm going up to my room."

"OK."

"Good night. See you in the morning," I said.

Krisann said, "Feel better."

"Thanks."

I grabbed my food and I was gone. I was happy to leave. I ate my dinner, drank some Nyquil, showered, and watched TV until I fell asleep.

—m—

Every day we would eat breakfast at the hotel restaurant and then head straight to the convention center. We would work all day and then go back to the hotel for dinner. I was so ready to go home.

The week was dragging. One morning I skipped breakfast and told Krisann I would meet her at the convention center. I needed to sleep a little bit more. When I woke up, I felt better. I showered, got dressed, grabbed some coffee in the restaurant, and took a cab to the convention center.

Everyone was all happy to see me. I brought them all coffee. The convention center was getting crowded, and buyers were looking around. We gave out line sheets and wrote some orders. Krisann was happy we wrote something, but she wasn't happy with the total number of orders. The line sucked, bottom line.

Thursday

It was everyone's last day at the show. Although I would be running the booth alone the next day, I was happy Krisann was leaving because all she did was bitch about not making enough sales. I just didn't want to hear it anymore. The convention center was not busy, but there were still people walking around.

Krisann asked, "So how much did we sell?"

Her mom totaled up the orders. "Well, Anita sold twenty thousand dollars, and Collin sold ten thousand dollars."

"Nice. Anita, you are the winner."

"Thanks. I'll try to sell more tomorrow while you guys are at the fashion show," I said.

I smiled at Collin, and he gave me a dirty look. I laughed and said, "Better luck next time, Cali."

"Yeah, next time, Brooklyn."

Krisann said, "We could have sold a lot more."

"Listen, Krisann, we did the best we could to sell the line," I said.

She stayed quiet.

"We opened up several new accounts that had never heard of us. They see the line has potential," I said.

I couldn't believe she was not happy with the sales. She had antici-pated making at least $100,000. Really? Krisann was out of her mind. In order to make $100,000 or better, a company had to advertise; the line had to be of good quality, and it had to be known. If people don't have a clue about the company, they will not buy the line—especially the major stores.

Krisann, Ms. Wright, and Collin left at 1:00 p.m. to catch their 4:00p.m. flight. I was alone all afternoon. I made a sale for $3,000. I knew Krisann probably wouldn't be happy, but a sale is a sale.

Five o'clock came, and I was already walking out of the convention center to catch a cab to the hotel. Once there I went to my room, showered, and dressed. I had dinner and a few drinks and then walked into the casino. I was hoping to leave with some money. I tried a slot machine. I played twenty dollars and lost it all. I went back to my room, put my pajamas on, and watched some TV before falling asleep.

I woke up feeling much better and took my time getting ready. I had some breakfast and coffee to go. I was happy it was Friday (TGIF). I was alone. That meant I had to pack and ship everything on my own. But I had shipped it all there myself, so it didn't make a difference.

The convention center was not crowded, but people were still coming in. I was happy that I was able to get a few more new customers with orders totaling $10,000. That was a lot more from where Krisann started.

At 3:00 p.m. I started packing because I had a 7:00 p.m. flight, and I had a lot to do.

A security officer approached me and said, "Excuse me, miss."

I looked up and said, "Yeah?"

"You can't start packing till five."

"Really? Why?" I asked.

"Those are the rules," he said.

"Yeah, OK."

When he left I continued to pack, but I left the clothing line on the grids. I had to go and get boxes from the shipping center to pack everything.

By 4:30 p.m. I didn't care. I took the line off the grids. But there were not enough carts to bring the boxes to UPS, and that delayed me. I had to wait until a cart was available. Finally I was able to take all the boxes and send them off. But Krisann didn't want me to ship the salesman cart because she didn't want to pay to ship it back to the office. So I had to take the squeaky, beat-up salesman cart with me on the plane.

I took a cab to the hotel. I showered, checked out, and headed to the airport. Everyone turned and stared at me as I walked through the airport with the squeaky-ass salesman cart. All I wanted to say to them was, "I know it squeaks. I know!"

When I got to the ticket agent's desk to check the cart, I placed it on a scale. It weighed more than a hundred pounds.

"You can send only packages that weight seventy pounds or fewer," said the agent. "I can give you boxes for the rest."

"OK," I said with a sigh.

I had to take stuff out of the salesman cart and put it in a box. As I stepped aside to pack and repack, I saw a man approaching me.

He smiled and said, "Hello."

"Yeah?" I said.

"How are you?"

"What do you want?"

"How are you doing?"

I laughed and then looked at the ticket agent. "Really?" I asked. I turned to the man and said, "Really?" I rolled my eyes, and I kept packing.

"Hmm," he said.

"Dude, really? You see I'm busy packing. If you're not going to help me, then step."

"Sorry," he said and walked away.

Once I finished packing, the ticket agent said, "Some nerve, huh?"

"Can you believe that? I'm trying to pack, and this asshole is trying to pick me up. All I want to do is go home."

"I have bad news for you."

"What?" I asked.

"You just missed your flight."

I started to cry. I was exhausted, and all I wanted to do was go home.

"Aww, don't cry," said the agent. "Please don't cry. I promise to get you on the next flight. How long have you been here? Were you here for Magic?"

"Yes, I was here for Magic. I've been here all week and believe me there is no magic about it," I said.

"You're from New York, right?"

"Yes, Brooklyn. Have you ever been to New York City?"

"No, but I'm dying to go."

"It's the city that never sleeps."

"Yes, I heard that," she said.

"It's always busy, with people walking around day and night. Let me know when you come, and I'll take you around."

"You would? Is it dangerous?"

"Yeah, it's dangerous, like every other city. You just have to be careful. Here, take my phone number."

"Awesome. Thanks." She looked around to make sure no one was listening and then came close to me. "Listen, you have been through shit today. So you're flying first class. Your plane leaves in two hours."

"Really?" I asked.

"Yes. You deserve it."

"Oh my God. Thanks. Don't forget to call me. See you in New York."

"You bet."

I had two hours to kill, so I bought some coffee. As I got it, I saw the asshole who had tried to talk to me. I walked toward the gate, found a seat, and waited for my flight. I hoped he didn't see me. I was happy I didn't have to lug that salesman cart around. I relaxed and people watched.

As the airline agent called my flight, I didn't get up too fast.

"First-class seats, please come forward. First-class seats, please come forward."

Oh shit. I was in first class! I smiled and then got up quickly and boarded the plane. A flight attended brought me to my window seat.

She took my carry-on and placed it in the overhead compartment for me.

"Can I get you a glass of champagne?" she asked.

"Yes, please, and keep them coming," I said.

She smiled and said, "Yes, ma'am."

Wow, first class was nice. I could get used to it.

"Ma'am, I would like to go over tonight's menu," said the attendant.

"Sure," I said.

"Would you like surf and turf or filet mignon?"

I smiled and said, "I'll take the surf and turf, please."

"More champagne?" she asked.

"Yes, please." I drank and ate everything that was offered. The best part was the dessert: tiramisu and cappuccino. Damn, that was how the wealthy lived? It was the good life. I couldn't go back to coach after all that service.

I slept for four hours straight. I woke up just in time for the landing. I got my luggage and walked off the plane.

Finally I was going home. There was a car waiting for me at the airport. When the driver dropped me off, I asked, "Oh, by the way, can you please take that noisy-ass, ghetto suitcase to the office tomorrow?"

"Sure, ma'am," he said.

"Thank you."

On Monday morning I was back in the office. I was happy to see Brandy and Keisha.

Brandy said, "Good morning, Anita. How was the trip?"

"Stressful. We have a lot to do because Krisann and Collin will be back with boxes of samples. Hopefully they sold the entire inventory they took with them."

Brandy said, "Remember, we have that event coming soon."

"Oh shit, that's right," I said.

"When is it?" Keisha asked.

"I don't know. Brandy, check the calendar."

She yelled from the office, "It's in two weeks."

"Damn. We have a lot to do," I said.

Keisha said, "Yeah, and we have to clean too."

We all laughed. The event was a Friday night after-work networking event. We were going to charge twenty dollars at the door, which included food, drinks, a fashion show, and shopping. There was so much to do.

—␣—

On the day of the event, Krisann, as always, waited till the last minute to get the food and the models. She was scrambling. The models were looking to get paid, and Krisann didn't want to pay, so they pulled out. It was so stressful and busy trying to get the office clean and pull together enough stock for the event. Finally we confirmed the food, models, and makeup. We used several of the vendors we'd used before: Touch and Go, Made in the Shade, and Lilly Fields, which sold paintings. The food came from Famous Sylvia's in Harlem.

The vendors started to arrive as we were getting everything ready.

Krisann said, "Anita, make sure the bathroom is clean and that there is enough tissue."

"Sure," I said. I looked at the girls and thought, *What the hell?*

I was talking to myself as I walked off, feeling pissed. I couldn't believe I had to clean the bathroom. That was bullshit. I never had to do shit like that before. I'd left one job because of the cursing, and I'd come here to clean. As I turned the corner to walk back to the bathroom, Keisha and Brandy were coming to get me.

"Who are you talking to?" Brandy asked.

I smiled and I said, "Myself."

We all laughed.

"OK. Let's get this event started." I said.

One of the models walked over. "Can I talk to you?" she asked me.

"Sure, what's up?"

"Am I getting paid for this?"

I looked at Brandy and Keisha. I wanted to laugh. "I don't know," I said. "What did Krisann tell you?"

"All she said was to come and model her new spring clothing line."

"OK. I don't handle that. You need to speak to her about that."

"OK, thanks," she said.

Krisann was cheap. She wanted everyone to work for free. People may have worked for free for the first event, but after that they wanted to get paid for their services. It was only fair. She didn't give away her merchandise for free, so why should anyone else?

Everyone was setting up, and the models were still arriving. The event was from 6:00 p.m. to 10:00 p.m. There were only four models and a makeup person. The food arrived, and the caterers started setting up.

Krisann asked, "How's it going, ladies? Do we have the table in the hallway set up?"

"Yes. Keisha is out there," I said.

"What about the inventory?"

"Inventory is in your room, folded nicely near the racks."

"OK. Thanks," Krisann said.

People started arriving. The models were getting made up and dressed. The food smelled so good. I had to make sure I ate before the savages got it all.

The show was about to start. Krisann took the microphone. "Hi, everyone. Thanks for coming. Please shop, eat, and watch the show."

Keisha, Brandy, and I toasted.

Brandy said, "Hope she makes money so we can get our checks this week."

Keisha said, "And that they don't bounce."

I did one of my deep sighs. Here I go again. "I know. Shut up."

It was pretty crowded. Everyone was eating, drinking, shopping, and enjoying the fashion show. I was happy that people were buying inventory. Everyone had a shopping bag. But by 10:15 p.m., I was ready to go home. I went looking for Krisann.

The makeup artist saw me and asked, "Hey, Anita, have you seen Krisann?"

"No, I'm looking for her, too," I said.

"I did the makeup and I want to get paid."

"Here she comes."

Krisann walked toward us. "What's up?"

"I'm leaving. See you on Monday," I said.

"OK. Thanks for everything. Before you leave can you please take all the trash to the freight elevator?"

"Yeah, sure," I said.

"Thanks," Krisann said.

I walked away. I threw the garbage toward the freight elevator and then left. I'd busted my ass at that event and all of the events, fixing the place and cleaning, and she didn't care.

Monday

While on the elevator riding up to the office, I prayed it would not be a mess. I was so pissed that Krisann had asked me to take out the garbage before I'd left the event. I opened the door, and to my surprise the office was clean. I was glad because I would have been pissed otherwise.

I heard the door open. It was Brandy and Keisha.

"Good morning," they said.

"Good morning. What time did you guys leave on Friday?" I asked.

"Is she here yet?" Brandy asked in a whisper.

I said, "No."

Brandy said, "I left at nine. You?" she asked Keisha.

Keisha said, "I left at nine thirty."

"Shit, I left at ten thirty, and she had the nerves to ask me to throw out the garbage before I left."

"Yeah, she's like that, and she's cheap."

"Oh, I know that."

Keisha said, "I'm going to clean the stockroom. It's a mess."

Brandy said, "OK. I'll vacuum the rug and then I'll be there to help you."

"Keisha, I'll help you, too," I said.

"OK."

Krisann walked in and peeked her head in the stockroom. "Good morning, ladies."

We said good morning.

I said, "Oh, Donald called, asking about the samples you used for the show."

"OK, thanks. I will call him," Krisann said.

"OK."

She walked to her office and closed her door. Brandy and I looked at each other.

I said, "Well, it's only Monday. Maybe things will get better."

Brandy said, "Every time she has her office door closed all day, it's a problem with money."

I said, "Yeah, I know. I'm looking for another job."

Brandy said, "Shh. Me too."

Keisha said, "Good, because she takes advantage of you."

I said, "Yeah, I know."

"You're the best thing that's happened to this company."

"Thank you, she can stay with her trophies."

We all laughed.

All week Krisann was behind her closed office door. She asked me to take messages. Everyone was calling: the models, the makeup artist, and the vendors. They all wanted their money.

Friday

Krisann came in with an attitude, slamming doors.

"Good morning. I don't want to be disturbed. Please take messages," she said.

"OK," I replied.

Brandy walked into the office. "I see she has her door closed."

"Yeah, I know. As soon as she walked in, she said no calls," I said.

"I need my check today."

"Me too."

As the day continued, we worked as if Krisann was not in the office.

"You wanna order Chinese food?" Brandy said.

I said, "Yeah, comfort food. I'm going to ask Krisann if she wants lunch. Also I can check out her attitude."

"Yeah, that's a good idea."

I knocked on Krisann's door.

"Come in," she said.

"We're ordering Chinese food. Do you want some?" I asked.

"No, I'm good. Thanks."

"OK."

"So did she have an attitude?" Brandy asked.

"Yup. She was on the phone," I said.

We ate lunch and continued to work. By 4:30 p.m. Krisann had not given us our checks. We would all be leaving the office at 5:00 p.m.

"OK, who's gonna knock on her door and ask for our checks?" Brandy asked.

I smiled and said, "Of course it's me, punk ass."

We laughed and looked at our watches. It was 4:59 p.m.

"Ready?" Brandy asked.

"Yeah, but you're coming with me," I said. "You knock, and I'll talk."

We had our coats on when we got to her door.

"OK. Ready?" Brandy asked.

We were laughing.

"No," I said.

Brandy had her fist ready to knock.

"Wait, wait." I took a deep breath. "OK, knock."

"Come in," Krisann said.

I looked at Brandy and then opened the door. "Hi, Krisann. We're leaving. Have a good weekend," I said.

"OK, you too."

Brandy and I looked at each other and then I said, "Do you have our checks?"

"Oh yeah, here," Krisann said.

We walked in, grabbed them, and then said good night.

"Good night, and please leave my office door open," Krisann said.

"OK."

We got out of there.

On the elevator Brandy said, "I'm going to cash my check across the street."

"Yeah, me too. I need some cash now," I said.

The check-cashing place was always crowded on Fridays after work. After about half an hour, we reached the cashier. We had our checks and IDs ready.

The cashier walked back and forth and then looked into a file cabinet. Then she went to talk to someone about the checks.

Brandy looked at me. "What's going on?"

"I don't know, but it doesn't look good," I said.

The cashier came back and handed us our checks and IDs. "I'm sorry. We cannot cash your checks."

"Why?" we asked.

"Her checks have bounced here several times."

We laughed and walked out.

I said, "This is not good."

Brandy said, "Damn."

"Now what?"

"Let me think...Let's go to that cashier place on Forty-Sixth and Seventh Avenue."

"OK. I hope they don't know her there."

We both laughed.

Brandy said, "Yeah, I know."

We headed to the other check-cashing place. It was crowded too.

"Damn, Anita! This place is worse," Brandy said.

"If this doesn't work, I'm going home."

"Me too."

"Let's pray we get them cashed here today."

As we got closer to the cashier, I could see that Brandy had her fingers crossed.

I said, "Girl, I have my toes crossed too."

We both laughed, and the cashier smiled at us. We handed her the checks and IDs, and then we held hands. We smiled at each other when the cashier started counting the cash.

We walked outside and hugged each other.

"This is bullshit. I can't continue like this. Krisann needs to set us up for direct deposit," I said.

"I know," Brandy said.

"Good night."

"Have a good weekend."

"You too."

—⁂—

Another Friday rolled around. Krisann had her door closed, and it was 4:45 p.m. I wanted to leave. Brandy and I looked at each other. Before I could say anything, Krisann came out of her office and gave us our checks.

"Have a good weekend, ladies," she said.

"We thanked her and wished her a good weekend too"

She walked out of the office, toward the bathroom. Brandy and I headed to the elevator. Brandy was about to say something, but I motioned with my hand for her to wait. As soon as we got into the elevator I said, "OK, you can talk now."

"She couldn't hear me," Brandy said.

"Yes she can, especially when the hallway is quiet. She can hear everything."

"I'm so happy we didn't have to knock on the door."

"Yeah, I know. Me too. You know, yesterday she asked me if I'm looking for a job."

"What did you tell her?" Brandy asked.

"I told her no. You think I'm going to tell her? I would be out of my mind. And the best part was when she said, You know, I can tell when people are lying to me.' I just looked dead into her eyes and told her I'm not looking."

"What did she say?"

"Nothing, but I did give my friend Denise my resume because she knew someone was looking for a Customer Service Rep. If this works out I'm going to take it." I said.

"Good. You deserve better. She takes advantage of you," Brandy said.

"I know."

My cell phone rang. "Hello."

"Hi, can I speak to Anita?"

"Speaking."

"Hi, Anita, I'm Nancy Lopez. I would like to meet up with you and discuss a customer-service position I have available."

"Sure. When?"

"How about Monday, one thirty?"

"OK. Where?"

"Do you know Arnos?"

"Yes I do, they are on Thirty-Eighth Street."

"Oh great, see you there"

"OK"

It was perfect because I could meet her while I was out to lunch. I think my interview suit needs to be retired. I wore heather tweed brown slacks with a camel cashmere long sleeve v-neck, brown leather blazer and brown leather pointy boots.

As soon as I walked into the restaurant, I looked for Nancy. She stood up and waved at me. She was already having a cocktail and waved at the waiter.

"Another one, please. Would you like a drink?" she asked me.

"Sure. A Coke, please," I said.

Nancy spoke about the job duties and looked over my resume. The company brought in containers of merchandise from China. Nancy was the sales rep for the fashion industry and the major department stores for New York and Los Angeles. I would handle customer service and inside sales for her customers. We spoke about salary and hours.

"So what do you think? Do you want the job?" she asked.

I said, "Yes, of course. I'm not afraid of hard work."

She smiled. "When can you start?"

"In two weeks. I have to give my job notice."

"OK. See you in two weeks."

"See you then."

We shook hands, and I left. I hoped this company would be different. I hoped I'd made the right choice.

After Krisann handed me my check that week, she said, "I've started direct deposit for you."

"Thanks, but I'm leaving the company," I said.

"You are? Why? I asked if you were looking, and you said no."

"I wasn't looking. It just came up."

"I'm sorry you're leaving," Krisann said.

"I know."

"Thanks for everything, Anita."

"You're welcome."

During my last two weeks at Willows, Krisann was not happy about my leaving, but she knew she was not able to pay my salary anymore.

I trained a girl for my position, and after two weeks I moved on.

Ten

SOS

SOS was the largest container cargo line in the United States. They supplied everyone in the fashion industry. They were located in the World Trade Center.

My position was customer-service inside-sales representative. This meant taking care of all her customers by tracking their containers that were being shipped by boat or train.

Nancy Lopez was Hispanic, about five two, around a size four, with short, brown hair. She had been married for two years but had no children, only a poodle named Lady. She had been with SOS for ten years. Nancy was on the road every day except Tuesdays.

My salary was pretty decent compared to that of someone who did not have experience. During my first day at SOS, I was busy learning the new system and filling out paperwork. Starting over again somewhere new and different was good. Both of my supervisors were women, Emily and Nancy. The big boss was a man, which didn't mean much if they influenced him.

I met so many people, I couldn't keep up with the names. There were a hundred people working at that office. It was a huge, open space.

I had never seen so many cubicles. They were waist high; everyone could see and hear everything. It was going to be interesting.

Emily supervised all of the sales reps and their assistants. She also took care of the time sheets, vacation, and so forth. Everything got mailed to the main office in Maine, where the corporate and Human Resources offices were located.

She was five one; Polish; heavyset; with over processed blond hair and glasses. She had been dating a fireman for years, and she was dying for him to marry her. She had been with SOS for fifteen years.

Dolores handled everything dealing with US Customs. She had a lot of porcelain dolls in her cubicle; she was a big-time collector. I didn't like them at all. Growing up I had always been afraid of porcelain dolls, and Dolores had several that really scared me. I was afraid that one day they would come alive, so I made many calls to Dolores instead of going over to her desk. She was a five-foot-tall Hispanic woman with salt-and-pepper hair. She had been with SOS for twenty years. I liked her because she said it like it was.

Janet was a newlywed. She was about five feet seven; Italian with long wavy hair. She was a nice girl and a hard worker. Janet was moving up to sales. She was training me for her old position. She was leaving on her honeymoon in four weeks. Janet had been with SOS for two years. I really liked her.

Two weeks of training, and after that I was on my own. I would also be assisting Janet with orders and customer support. I didn't like what I did, but it was a job. There were a few more customer-service sales assistants who did the same thing I did but worked for other sales reps.

Nicole did the same thing I did, but her sales reps were great and hardly bothered her for anything. She was also a hard worker. She was young, about twenty-two years old; five three; Italian with long, brown hair. She lived with her parents. We got along and went out to lunch together. She had been there for two months.

One day Nancy and Vivian walked in laughing like high school girls. Nicole and I looked at each other. There was a row of four cubicles on each side. That made eight altogether. Nicole was in a cubicle that was in front of me but on the other side.

Vivian was Nancy's pet. She would take care of Nancy's expenses and run her personal errands. Vivian was married with children and had been with SOS for twelve years.

After I'd worked at SOS for a month, my sales reps invited me out for drinks. I was surprised. I really didn't want to go, but I'm a team player. It would be the first and last time I would go out for drinks with those women. I was very quiet because I didn't know them well. I just smiled and observed. Nicole didn't go because it was supposed to be just me and my sales reps: Nancy, Emily, Vivian, and Janet. I guess it was a way to break the ice.

We found a booth, and before sitting down Emily and Nancy called the waiter over for us to order drinks. They whispered stupid things to each other like schoolgirls; It was so annoying. They were all so phony except for Janet. There was nothing she could do but sit there and pretend their jokes were funny.

I couldn't wait until the night was over. I kept looking at my watch. I was still on my first drink when Emily was calling the waiter over for another round. When he got to the table, I stood up.

"Ladies, good night," I said.

Nancy said, "Where are you going?"

"I gotta go."

"Have another drink," Nancy said.

"No, but thanks for everything."

Nancy and Emily looked at me and said bye.

I put a twenty-dollar bill on the table next to Janet. "Have a good weekend."

As I walked out, I saw Vivian walking back to the table. I pretended I didn't see her, but it didn't matter because she was always in la-la land.

My job was easy, and I picked it up quickly. I was already handling customers who called all day, every day about their shipments and other problems.

I arrived at the office at 8:30 a.m. and started eating my breakfast when Nancy called me from her cell phone, but I didn't answer it because I didn't officially start my workday until 9:00 a.m. I had enough time to eat and then start the day, so I continued eating.

As I was finishing my breakfast, I saw Emily walking my way. What did she want?

"What's going on with the Conway order?" she asked.

She didn't even say good morning. Nancy must have told her I was already in.

"Good morning," I said.

"Oh, I'm sorry. Good morning."

"What's the question?"

"Was it shipped? Talk to Nancy," Emily said, "she's on the phone."

I picked up the phone. "Hello," I said to Nancy.

"What's going on with the Conway order? Was it shipped?"

Smiling, I said, "Let me check." I heard her huffing and puffing. She was saying to someone else, "I can't believe it didn't fucking go out."

"OK...Let me see...." I was stalling because I didn't like her tone of voice. She was talking shit. "It was delivered yesterday at five thirty and signed for by Morgan."

"OK." She hung up without saying thanks. Sigh.

I looked at Emily's desk. She was answering her phone. As she started talking, she looked in my direction. I stared dead at her, and she quickly turned the other way. I knew she was talking to Nancy about me. I'm glad the order had shipped because Nancy had never mentioned anything to me about Conway's order. I'm sure if it hadn't shipped, she would have blamed me for it. All of that was too familiar. There was always someone around to ruin things. I was on that ride again.

Later that afternoon Nancy and Vivian walked into the office with shopping bags. They were laughing like high school girls. Nancy stopped by Emily's office. I pretended not to see them and continued working. I was sure things would not end well for me.

Nancy had to pass my desk to get to her corner cubicle. "Hi," she said.

"Hello." I gave her a smirk as if to say, "Bitch, I got your number."

Dolores came over to my desk and handed me some paperwork. "I can't stand her."

"Who?" I said.

"Your boss."

"Which one?"

We both laughed.

"I can't stand Nancy. You know, she's Puerto Rican, but she thinks she's white," Dolores said.

"People will be people," I said.

"Be careful with her."

"I know," I said.

"The other one thinks her shit don't stink. Fat bitch."

"I saw that too, and she's a snob. When I ask her for help, she sighs. So I don't bother her anymore."

"Yes, she's known for that and other things."

We both laughed.

"We should go out to lunch one day," Dolores said.

I said, "OK."

—◠◠—

The company was having a dinner for some clients, sales and their assistants had to attend. They wanted the clients to know everyone working on their accounts.

It was so boring, and I was so ready to leave. I didn't say much during dinner. I just observed everyone. Nancy was tipsy. She was all over one of the clients like a tramp. They first ordered drinks and then appetizers and then dinner. I wanted to leave, but they ordered coffee and dessert too. They were so phony. I was so over that job. After several months things were going OK. But I was still not comfortable there and I didn't trust any of them.

The Christmas Party

There was so much going on with shipping, entering orders, and new contracts, but Nancy and Emily were busying planning the company Christmas party. You would have thought they were planning their prom.

The party was held at a restaurant, in a private party room. Several clients were invited. I stayed for only about two hours. Vivian and Emily were on the dance floor with clients while holding on to their wine glasses.

While I was getting my coat, I heard some noise. I looked through the coats and found Nancy getting it on with one of the sales guys from Calvin Klein, but they never saw me. I'd heard she was screwing the clients, but I hadn't thought it was true. Maybe that was how she kept them happy. If business got bad, she could always move to Vegas.

I was going to say good night to the others, but Emily had her head on the table, probably from drinking too much. I didn't see the other girls, so I left. I wouldn't be missed anyway.

—⚉—

January was when clients renewed their contracts. Nancy always freaked out during this busy season and for nothing because as long as she kept the clients *happy*, SOS would always be in business.

One day Nancy was out on sales calls. She left me a note that said, "Hey, Anita, can you fax the contract over to Neiman Marcus? It's on my desk. Thanks, Nancy."

Wow. She said thanks. I was sure she would be calling me all day. I found the Neiman Marcus folder on her desk. There was a blank contract and a cover sheet in it, ready to be faxed.

I faxed the contract. I placed the confirmation sheet and the other papers back on her desk and continued to do my job. I faxed a few more contracts for Vivian and waited for the confirmations. I noticed there was no paper, so I added more paper, and the faxes were coming out like crazy. There were five pages waiting to be printed.

I sorted the faxes for Dolores and Nicole and placed them in their boxes. Before I walked away, another fax came through. I stopped and waited for it.

Hi, Lopez,
I got the contract, but if you want it signed you have to come to Los Angeles. Don't forget to bring the lingerie I bought you. I can't wait to see you, and I have that pot you like to smoke.
Love, Frosty

I turned red as if the note was written to me. Oh my God. She was not only a tramp but a pothead too.

I wasn't sure what to do about the fax. I ripped it up and then I taped it back and then I made a copy and stuffed it into my purse. I didn't want to leave any evidence that I'd had it.

Half an hour later, Emily walked over to me. "Hey, Anita, everything OK?"

"Yes," I said.

"Everything OK?" she asked again.

"Yes, everything is OK. Are you OK?" I knew what she was fishing for.

"By the way, are we getting signed contracts back?"

"No," I said.

"Did you check the fax machine to make sure there's paper?"

I smiled and said, "Yes."

"OK, thanks."

As soon as Emily walked to her desk, my phone rang.

"Good afternoon, Anita speaking."

"Did you get a reply?"

It was Nancy. She was probably looking for her letter.

"From whom?"

"Anita! This is Nancy!"

"Yes, I know."

"Did you fax the contract to Neiman Marcus?" she asked.

"Yes."

"To Mr. Frost?"

"Yes, to Mr. Frost," I said.

"Did he fax the contract back?"

"No."

"How do you know?"

"All I received was the confirmation that the contract was received. I placed it on your desk."

"He didn't fax anything?" Nancy asked.

"No, but I will keep checking."

"No! Don't worry about it." She hung up.

That afternoon Dolores and I were working on some customs issues at my desk when Nancy walked into the office with her dog, Lady. She stopped by Emily's desk to show her Lady. Dolores and I stopped what we were doing because Emily was carrying on so loudly about the dog. We looked at each other.

"Here comes Lady and the tramp," I said.

Dolores and I just laughed.

"She sure is a lady," Dolores said.

"She sure is a tramp," I said.

"You're crazy, Anita. See you later."

"Bye."

—⚋⚋—

From where I sat, I could kind of see everything. Nicole was on my left, and there were two other people in front of me. There was a walkway and then Emily's desk. Emily sat in front of the big boss's office. His name was Kevin Burger.

Kevin Burger had worked for SOS for about eight years. He seemed nice, but I rarely had to deal with him.

Vicky was the new girl. She sat two cubbies in front of me. She was about five ten, with red hair—pretty and not too bright.

I walked into the storage/copy room, where the fax and copy machines were. Vicky and Emily were busy making copies and faxing. Emily was showing Vicky how to use the copy and fax machines.

"Hi, ladies," I said.

They both said hello. I was picking up some folders for my files.

"Thanks, Emily," Vicky said.

"Sure; anytime, Vicky. I'm here to help you as much as you need."

She never said that to me, but whatever.

Emily was so helpful to Vicky because she was tall and had pretty, red hair. You would have thought Emily was in love with her. She was catering to Vicky's every need; it was embarrassing. I heard she even paid for Vicky's lunch.

There was one woman whose cubicle I had to pass to get to the kitchen: Jeannie.

Jeannie was in her sixties. I think she was ready to retire. She had been with the company for twenty-five years.

Every day I greeted her, and she would always curse. Every time she'd pass my desk, she would say, "Anita." I would look up, and she would say, "What the fuck are you looking at?"

I would die laughing. "At you, crazy lady," I would say.

She would laugh and say, "Good morning."

"Good morning, Jeannie. How are you?"

"Ready to retire from this hellhole."

We would both laugh.

"You're funny," I said.

"Don't forget crazy."

I would laugh so hard, tears would come out of my eyes. "You see? You know?"

"See you later, Anita."

"OK."

———※———

It was Tuesday, and Nancy was in the office. She was walking around like she was on speed.

Nicole turned to me and asked, "What's up with her?"

I opened my eyes wide. "I don't know."

We both laughed.

I needed some more coffee. I passed Jeannie's desk, and she threw me a paper clip.

I turned and faced her. "Did you just throw me a paper clip?"

"Yes, bitch, I did."

I walked over to her desk. "Come here. Let me see something. You have something behind your head." I started to check the back of her head, under her hair.

Jeannie moved away from me. "What the fuck are you doing?"

I laughed and then said, "I'm looking for those three sixes on the back of your head."

We both just died laughing.

"And you call me crazy," she said.

I said, "You are. See you later."

———※———

Every week I would work on a report for Nancy on shipping schedules for each customer. After she approved it, I would e-mail it to the customers. I gave up asking Emily for help because she would sigh like she was annoyed when I asked her a question. I wasn't the only one she did that to; she was that way with everyone. After she gave me major attitude, I never bothered her again.

Once I sent a report that was incorrect to one of the clients, and Nancy had a fit. She never told me I had made a mistake. She should have come to me if there was a problem, but she never did. Instead she bitched to Emily and Vivian about it. How was I supposed to fix the problem if she wouldn't address it or if I didn't know I'd made a mistake?

On Fridays Emily would always be busy filling out the time sheets and sending them to the main office in Maine. That was where the entire payroll was done. I heard she had been fixing the time sheets for years. When she was out of the office, or when she took a long weekend, Emily wrote on her time sheet that she had been in the office. When she couldn't go on vacation, she cashed it in. She would sign in at 7:00 a.m. and leave at 4:00 p.m.

That Friday afternoon I was right behind Emily and Nancy. They jumped onto the elevator knowing I was behind them and closed the doors fast. I heard them giggling. Bitches. I really didn't want to be with them on the elevator anyway.

When I looked down, I saw an envelope for the Maine office. I opened it, and, to my surprise, there were the time sheets. Emily had been logging on hers that she worked from 7:00 a.m. to 8:00 p.m., but I saw her leaving every day at 4:00 p.m. Wow, it was true. She was scamming the company for four extra hours a day, that was twenty extra hours a week. How would the Maine office know if she stayed late?

I took Emily and Nancy's time sheets out and put them in my purse. I was going to throw them out in Brooklyn. I dropped them into a mailbox shoot. They would see a difference on their checks the following week. They were two catty bitches. I knew my days are numbered at SOS.

The following week I was called into Kevin's office. Emily was already there. I knew what was coming.

"OK, let's have it," I said.

Kevin said, "Unfortunately things are not working, and we have to relieve you of your duties."

"Why? What did I do wrong?" I knew the deal. I just wanted to see if he would say anything to me.

"We just decided this is not working out."

"Fine, but first let me say that I know I made some mistakes. However, Nancy should have spoken to me. Every time I would go to her"—I pointed at Emily—"she would always sigh or huff and puff with an attitude. How can I ask for help when she does that? And she does that with everyone."

Emily was stunned. Her mouth was open; she couldn't believe I'd said that. I turned and looked at her.

"Yes, you do that to everyone here. That's why no one asks you for help. You guys are notorious for throwing people under the bus."

Kevin said, "I'm sorry you feel like that."

"Well, I do. Is that all?" I asked.

"Yes."

I took my check and walked out. At my desk I grabbed my purse and coat and then walked over to Nicole.

"Where are you going?" she asked.

I whispered, "They fired me."

"What?"

I hugged her and said, "Here's my number. Keep in touch. Bye."

I walked over to Dolores and Jeannie and said my good-byes.

Nicole walked with me to the elevator. "What did they say?" she asked.

"All they said was that it wasn't working. I told them Emily has an attitude whenever she's asked a question."

"You did? Good, maybe she will change?."

"I doubt it. They're all nitwits."

We hugged, and she said, "Take care, and call me."

"I will."

I went back to working on my handbag line and made some money while looking for a job. Some of my clients were buying their bags from China, so it slowed down for me. I made some more calls and kept sending my résumé out.

A few days later, I got an e-mail from Donald, telling me that one of the divisions where he worked was looking for someone to do data entry. I said I'd do it.

Eleven

4 Apparel

I interviewed with 4 Apparel . The huge company purchased clothing licenses. They had about fifteen of them and manufactured all sorts of outerwear (wool, leather, fur coats and jackets); pants; skirts; and even team sport jackets and jerseys. It was a perfect time to sell jerseys because they were hot. The company also developed a few of its own brands. Eighty percent of the business was licensed name brands.

I could use some new coats, especially because they were name brand. I already had imagined a closet filled with down, leather, and wool coats and jackets. Every year 4 Apparel had a huge sample sale and I couldn't wait.

The position was for product data entry, which meant entering styles and orders for production. Donald from Willows also worked for 4 Apparel, as a production manager for the sports-license division.

Two girls interviewed me: Cheryl and Dawn. I would be taking over Dawn's position; she was moving to the IT department. Cheryl would be my backup. I would also be working with her on styles and color codes. They wanted to make sure I was a good fit for the position.

Cheryl and Dawn wanted me to meet my boss, Edith. She also interviewed me, and I heard afterward that she didn't want to hire me. She wanted to hire someone else, but the decision wasn't up to her. It was up to Dawn and Cheryl, and they really liked me.

Cheryl had been with the company for nine years. She handled all EDI (electronic data interchange): orders are sent electronically from the accounts.

Dawn had been with the company for three years and was moving to the IT department.

Edith asked me several questions and then said, "Give me a minute."

"OK," I said.

She walked out. A few minutes later, she walked back in and sat down. "So when can you start?"

"I can start in a week."

"Perfect. See you next week," she said.

"Thank you."

We shook hands, and I left.

Edith was the director of production, and she oversaw every division. She wore her hair in curly shag that was outdated and well-manicured nails that were always polished in burgundy. She'd been with 4 Apparel for more than fifteen years.

I never really had to work with Edith. I only had to ask her for vacation approval. I was basically on my own, which I loved because there was no one on my back. I did my job, and I did it well. If I did not do my job, everyone would have known because their styles and orders would not have been in the system. I entered orders for twelve divisions, and I had twelve different attitudes to deal with. Most of the people were cool, but some were not.

For the first year, things went well. The company offered medical and dental insurance and a 401(k) plan. The offices were on Seventh Avenue between Thirty-Eighth and Thirty-Ninth Streets. The company occupied five floors, and all day I was up and down, getting orders and style corrections. I had to make many calls because many of the styles didn't match the fabric codes that made up the style. I was happy there.

On my floor I had a basket where everyone placed their style masters and orders for me to enter. I had three days to enter them.

Margaret was one of the production coordinators for her division. She would put her orders on top of all the others so her division got entered first. I had been wondering why her division was always first, but then I saw her do it. I pretended not to see her. I waited until the third day to enter all of her stuff. She was very pushy and demanding. I didn't like that.

Margaret left the company and then came back (she should have stayed away). She was heavy and a nosy bitch.

Once, as I picked up all the orders and style setups from the basket, I saw Margaret coming my way with papers in her hands. She wobbled when she walked.

"Hi, Anita," she said.

"Hi, Margaret."

"Did you enter my orders?"

"No," I said.

"Why not? I put them in the basket four days ago."

"No, you didn't. I have three days, and today is the third day. They will be entered today."

She pressed her lips together and said, "OK."

That was not the first time Margaret had asked me to enter her orders first. I had done it before as a courtesy, but she was taking advantage of me. I entered the orders as they came: first come, first served.

Fifteen minutes later my phone rang. It was Edith.

"Hi, Anita. Can you come to my office?"

"Sure. I'll be right over." Now what?

When I walked into Edith's office, Margaret was already sitting there, and I knew the meeting was about her orders.

Edith said, "Please, come in."

I sat down. "Hello, Margaret."

"Hello, Anita," she replied.

"Hold on. I need to finish sending this e-mail." Edith loved hitting the keyboard with her burgundy-polished nails. "OK, I'm done. It has come to my attention from Margaret that you are taking too long entering orders. Is that true? Do you need someone to help you?"

"No, I have it under control. I told Margaret I have three days to enter orders, and her order was entered today."

Edith turned to Margaret. "Did you know about the three days?"

Margaret nodded.

"Yes, I told her about the three days," I said.

"Well, why beat a dead horse? Thanks, Anita," said Edith.

I walked out and went back to my desk.

One day I dropped off some orders Edith needed to see. She was eating cake. I'd had some earlier.

Every Monday Ed baked something for everyone on his floor. It was the best floor to work on, and I was glad I was on it.

"Oh my God, that cake is delicious." I said.

She immediately picked up the phone and placed a call. "Hey, Ed. Anita is in here trying to get the cake recipe from me."

My jaw dropped. After she hung up and looked at me, I said, "Here are the orders you needed. Oh, and thanks. I'll make sure to get the recipe from Ed."

She had the nerves to outright lie about the recipe. She was nothing but a wolf in sheep's clothing. As soon as I walked out of her office, I went straight to Ed's desk.

Ed had been with 4 Apparel for twelve years as a production coordinator for one of the well-known brand-name women's outerwear divisions.

As soon as he saw me, he started laughing. I shook my head.

"What the hell? I went to drop off some orders she needed, and then I bragged about your cake. She immediately called you, and she had the nerve to say I was trying to get it from her."

Ed was laughing hysterically. "She's known for that. First you have to tell her, 'Don't say anything.' Then you tell her what you want to say."

"Yeah, I know that now," I said.

We had to be careful when talking to Edith because if we complained to her about a colleague, she would immediately call that person into her office while we were sitting there. Before we could say anything, she would be telling the colleague about the complaint. We had to tell Edith not to say anything before we started talking.

After I got back to my desk, my phone rang. It was Dawn.

"Hi, Dawn. What's up?" I asked.

"Edith just called me about the orders. Do you need help?"

I laughed. "I told her I have it under control. Margaret started bitching to her that I'm taking too long. I told Margaret I have three days to enter them."

"Oh, that's why Edith was asking me about the three days. I'm so happy I don't have to work with her. She's such a bitch. Let me warn you."

"Yeah, I already know that," I said.

"And another thing. She didn't want to hire you," Dawn said.

"Really?"

"Yeah, but it wasn't her decision. It was Cheryl's and my decision, and we made a good one."

"Well, thank you, and yes, you did make a good decision," I said.

We both giggled.

—◊◊—

A few weeks later, I got an e-mail from Margaret:

> Hi Anita,
> I know you have been very busy, but can you please, please do me a huge favor and enter five styles and orders today?

I had been very busy, but I replied yes.

As I entered her orders, I found three that had problems. I went to see Margaret, but she was not in, so I spoke to her assistant, Hy.

Hy was the owner's only son. Margaret was teaching him about production. He was just out of law school; he'd failed the bar exam five times. He was there to learn the business.

Two days later I received an e-mail from Margaret. When I read it, I was livid. She'd had the nerve to copy Edith and Galinda too. She wrote:

> What happened to the orders I asked you to enter? They are missing. Anita, please read below as to your e-mail stating you would enter all five orders. You entered only two. What happened?

Galinda was the vice president of sales. She worked closely with Edith. She was a nice woman and very professional. She always had on amazing, expensive diamond jewelry.

I had to wait a bit before I answered Margaret's e-mail because if I didn't, I would curse her out. I stepped outside for a minute, and when I got back I wrote:

> Margaret, I tried entering the other three orders, but you didn't have the correct fabric codes for your styles. I spoke to Hy about it. And let me remind you that I did you a favor by entering your orders first.

I also copied Edith and Galinda on my reply. What a bitch. Margaret was trying to get me in trouble, and that was not right.

Ten minutes later I received another e-mail from her saying she was sorry, but she sent it to only me; she didn't copy Galinda or Edith.

That afternoon, while I was picking up my orders, Margaret stopped me and said, "Listen, Anita, I'm sorry about the e-mail. I didn't know."

"I guess you know now, huh?" I didn't even bother to ask why she had copied Edith and Galinda on the e-mail; it had backfired anyway. But now I knew I had to be careful with her and cover my ass.

—m—

I had been at 4 Apparel for three years, and my closet had been invaded by the beautiful coats and awesome jackets the company made. Every season I couldn't stop shopping. I love coats. I bought them in all kinds of fabric: wool, leather, down, and even a few furs. The samples were my size, and sometimes certain divisions used me as their fit model. I got a lot of samples for free, and I bought a lot at the sample sales. I had so many coats that I had to sell some because they would not all fit in my closet.

On every floor there was a cleaning lady, and they worked very hard. The company occupied floors thirty through thirty-five. There were spiral stairs connecting the thirtieth floor all the way to the thirty-fourth, but we had to take the elevator up to the thirty-fifth. On each floor there were several divisions, showrooms, salespeople, production, design, and so on. The owner, president, assistants, and several sales-people were on the thirty-fifth floor.

Adam was the owner of 4 Apparel. He had been in business for more than thirty years. He hoped his son, Hy, would take over the family business.

I was on the thirty-fifth floor, picking up several corrections on an order, when I heard someone yelling. As I walked toward the kitchen, I saw Michele yelling in the face of one of the cleaning ladies, Carmen.

"Are you an idiot? What is your problem?" Michele was pointing at the floor underneath the refrigerator. "I told you to clean that."

Then she mushed Carmen's face. I was stunned. I couldn't believe she'd done that. I was about to step in and stop it ,but I caught myself. Michele looked at me as if she thought I would say something, but I didn't, and neither did she. I gave her a look of disgust, shook my head, and walked away. I wish she would mush me. I would beat the crap out of her. Fucking bitch.

Carmen cleaned underneath the refrigerator with tears in her eyes. I was so pissed because I couldn't do or say anything about it. Maybe Carmen was working in the states illegally. Either way I couldn't get involved. It was not my fight.

Michele was Adam's assistant. She was in charge of the cleaning ladies, and they all hated her. Michele was a tall, tacky blonde. She wore high-heeled shoes with dress shorts. She looked like a prostitute.

Michele would always come to see Margaret. They gossiped about everyone in the office, especially Adam. Every time he went on vacation, Margaret would ask Michele all sorts of questions, from the cost of his trip to the type of bathroom soap in his hotel room. She was obsessed with his money and lifestyle.

—⟋⟍—

Once I was having a problem with my system, and Dawn was not answering her phone, so I decided to go and see her. As I started walking toward her, I saw her walking out of her office.

"Hey, I was just coming down to see you," Dawn said.

"Good, because I was coming to get you."

"How's it going?"

"Good, but I want to show you an error I got."

"OK."

As we waited by the elevators, Jennifer joined us.

"Hello, ladies," she said.

We both said hello.

Jennifer was the president of the company and had been for fifteen years. She was very pretentious and full of shit. She drew her power from belittling her employees.

As we enter the elevator, Jennifer looked me up and down. I looked back at her. She smiled and then checked out Dawn. Before we stepped out of the elevator, Jennifer said, "Lose the shoes."

"Huh?" Dawn asked. "What was that?"

"I said lose the shoes," Jennifer said and then the elevator doors closed.

I chuckled, and I looked at Dawn's shoes. She had on fake Louis Vuittons.

"Did she say lose the shoes?" I asked.

"Yeah. That fucking bitch. She always has something to say about what someone is wearing. Did you see how she looked at us? She always does that. I can't stand her. She thinks she's better than everyone. I can't stand her."

I felt bad for Dawn. Jennifer had no right to comment on her shoes. As the president of a large company, Jennifer should have been more professional; she shouldn't have criticized the people who worked for her. She should have criticized Michele when she came to work in shorts and high heels. As long as Dawn's feet got her to work, who cared what was on them?

After four years of entering orders, I wanted to do something else. I spoke to Edith about going into production. There were three production managers: Margaret, Shelia, and Donna, who all needed an assistant. I was hesitant to work with them because of the experiences I'd had with each of them.

Margaret would be very abusive, and Edith would turn her cheek. Shelia would work me to death and work late hours because that's how she works. And Donna…She was all right, but sometimes she was a bit pushy and had an attitude. She swore she knew everything.

Carl was an older man who had worked at 4 Apparel for a total of twelve years. After five years he had left the company and then come back. He handled freight containers coming in.

Carl and I sat next to each other for a couple of years. He did his work, and I did mine.

"Carl, I'm going into production".

"Good for you and who will you be working with?".

"Donna".

"I hate her, but I totally understand why you chose her. Good luck." Carl said.

"Thanks. I'm going to need it."

It was done. I would be working with Donna as her production assistant. Edith placed an ad in *Women's Wear Daily* for someone to fill my old position. Donna referred a friend, and someone from the IT department referred his wife.

My phone rang, and I saw Edith's name. I answered the phone. "Good morning, Edith."

"Good morning, Anita. I have two ladies I would like you to interview for your position."

"OK."

"When you're done, come see me, and let me know what you think," she said.

"OK."

I interviewed Donna's friend, Susan, and Fema, the IT guy's wife. Susan was a better fit because she knew the business, had entered orders for years and speaks english well. Fema had never entered an order, although anyone could be trained to do the job. She had no clue about the fashion industry; she spoke very low, and her English was not good. I kept asking her to repeat what she was saying. I did not have a clue what she was talking about, so all I did was nod my head.

I knocked on Edith's door and she said, "Come in."

I sat down.

"What do you think?" she asked.

"I think Susan is a better candidate for this position," I said.

"Why not Fema? You know she was an engineer in her country?"

"Fema's English is not good. I really couldn't understand what she was saying. She would have to work with a lot of divisions."

"She's an engineer," Edith repeated.

"If she's an engineer then why is she trying to work here?" I asked.

"Well, why beat a dead horse? Thank you, and I'll make a decision soon."

"OK."

Why ask for my opinion when it really didn't matter, nitwit. "She's an engineer, she's an engineer"—that was all Edith said. She might have been an engineer in her country, but that didn't mean anything at this company. She was too smart for the stupid position.

As I was walking over to my desk, I heard, "Anita, Anita." I looked, and it was Donna calling me over.

Sigh. "What's up?" I asked.

"Do you think she's going to hire my friend, Susan?" Donna asked.

I looked at her and chuckled. "No."

"No? Why? And why are you laughing? Tell me what happened."

"She's going to hire the tech's wife, but it's not going to work," I said.

"How do you know?"

"You'll see. I'll see you later." I walked away.

"OK."

Donna had been with the company for a few years. She was married with children. Her division was a high-end brand that manufactured outerwear for men and women in both cloth and leather.

After I spent a few months training Fema, she was on her own but, she was constantly calling me and coming over to my desk. I didn't mind because she really needed help, and I felt sorry for her. Everyone else was calling me and complaining they couldn't understand her. She would not last long. But she was an engineer....

Donna was disappointed that Edith had not hired Susan. "You know, Edith was wrong in not hiring Susan. She is well qualified. Instead Edith hired a bumbling idiot who can't speak English."

"That's what I told her. I said Susan has experience. Also, be careful with Edith," I said.

"What do you mean?" Donna asked.

I smiled. "She's a wolf in sheep's clothing."

"Really? I don't see that. She's a great person."

"You will," I said and left it at that.

—ıɯ—

As I worked with Donna, things were going well. I thought production would be stressful, but it was easy. I had to be organized, or things would fall through the cracks, and there would be delays. It took a lot to make a garment. Depending on the type there might be buttons, zippers, lining, pattern, sketches, and other things that went into the product, and it had to be done right.

I learned so many things. Not from Donna but on my own. She didn't show me how she handled her production. I asked questions and looked at the spec sheets and e-mails she placed in her book. She always gave me bullshit work to do, and she never went through the steps with me.

Donna had been working on the folder she'd created for production. It opened up and showed everything a garment needed to be produced, including the sketches and samples of whatever zipper, button, or other items that were needed to complete the garment.

I had never known she was creating the folder because she'd never involved me in anything. Now she was meeting with Edith about it.

"I'll be with Edith in her office," Donna said.

"OK."

Carl walked over to my desk and pointed toward Donna's. "Where's the bitch?"

I pointed to Edith's office. "With the other bitch."

We both laughed.

"Did you see the infamous folder?" he asked.

"I heard Donna talking about them, but I never saw them".

"People are saying it's a waste of time and no one will use it. Be careful with her".

"I will, thanks".

—◆—

When Donna got back, she said, "Anita, I want to show you a folder I created. Everyone in production will be using it."

I opened it and said, "Nice."

"The folder will make things easier. All you have to do is open it, and voilà—you have all the information you need for that one style."

I said, "Very nice."

She kept bragging all day about her folder. The folder. The folder. The folder. All I did was nod my head and smile.

—◆—

As time passed, I noticed that when I would come back from lunch Donna would always look at the clock on her computer. She also did that every morning. I made sure I was always on time, and I always took an hour lunch—no more, no less.

She hardly went out to lunch. Maybe that was why she was not happy when I went out. I had the right to a lunch break whether she liked it or not.

—◆—

Carl came over to work with Donna.

"Hey, Anita, how's it going with the laughing cow?" he asked.

"You're in a good mood," I said.

"I will be after I finish with the bitch. By the way, where the hell is she?"

"I don't know. She doesn't tell me anything. Oh, here she comes. Good luck."

"Yeah, thanks."

We both laughed. Once Donna and Carl saw each other, she immediately got an attitude. I didn't know why because he was a nice man.

—ɯ—

Every time the phone rang, it was Fema needing help. I was swamped, helping her fix the problems she was causing. Donna was catching an attitude with me about it. Instead of saying she didn't want me to help Fema, she stopped talking to me. So I ignored her and did my work.

Once I left my desk to go help Fema, but I didn't want Donna to know. I thought it was unfair of her to get mad at me for it. Maybe she was mad because the company hadn't hired Susan. Either way it was unprofessional of her to be upset with me.

Fema and I walked over to Shelia's office to show her the incorrect orders she had given. As we approached Shelia's area, I heard her talking to Hy about a sample.

"You have to follow the sample until it hits the warehouse," Shelia said.

"How do you spell warehouse?" Hy asked.

"W-a-r-e-h-o-u-s-e."

That's when we walked into her office. He was a nitwit and he is supposed to run the company one day. Scary.

I looked and Hy then smiled at Shelia. She smiled back. We discussed the orders and then Fema and I went back to work.

Shelia produced a high-end name brand line for men and women. She had been with the company for twelve years. Shelia was showing Hy the ropes on the high end division.

I returned to my desk and started a report that Donna needed. I saw Fema heading my way.

Donna got up and said to me, "I will handle this."

"Handle what?" I asked.

"Fema."

"Hello, Donna," Fema said then turned to me and said, "Hi, Anita. Can I show you—?"

Donna cut her off. "No, Fema from now on you have to ask me first because Anita works with me now."

I saw Fema's face turn all shades of red.

"OK," she said then walked away with her head down. I felt so bad for Fema. There was no need for Donna to talk to her like that.

"This is gone way too far. From now on if anyone needs your help they are going to have to ask me first," Donna said.

"All right, but maybe you should send an e-mail out to everyone about that," I said.

"Yes, I will do that."

Oh my God. What have I gotten myself into? What was I supposed to say? I should have stayed where I was or I regret the move? I was happy going into production, but I would not do it again. I hoped coming to work for Donna wasn't a bad idea.

"Oh, Anita, did you send that e-mail to the corporate office regarding the samples?"

"Yes."

"When?"

"Yesterday."

"I never got an e-mail."

"I copied you on the e-mail."

"When? I didn't get it."

I checked my e-mails. I not only printed a copy of the e-mail, but I also forwarded Donna the e-mail.

"Here," I said.

"What's this?" Donna asked.

"The e-mail you said I didn't copy you on."

"Oh, OK. Thanks."

When she walked away I turned off her computer because she was being a bitch. When Donna sat down she moved her mouse around. "Oh, damn," she said. "What happened to my computer?"

I didn't even turn around, I continued working and I pretended not to hear her. She sat right behind me and she could see everything I did on my computer. I didn't care because I did my work.

"Did your computer turn off?" Donna asked.

I didn't turn around when I answered her. "What?"

"My computer went off somehow, did yours?"

"No," I said.

"OK, I need to get this checked out."

Every time she got bitchy with me I would turn her computer off. The phone rang. It was Edith. "Hi, Edith," I said.

"Hi, Anita, is Donna there?," Edith said.

"She's at her desk."

"Oh, I thought I was calling her desk. Thank you, I will call her."

Donna hung up from speaking with Edith. She got up and said, "I'll be with Edith if anyone is looking for me."

"OK."

It was so much better when she was not around. Donna was always lurking around to see what I was up to.

I was leaving for the day and Donna was still with Edith. I was going home. Tomorrow was another day. I left her a note: "Good night, see you in the morning."

The next day as I walked into the office I didn't see Donna at her desk and I didn't see her belongings. As I sat at my desk I saw Edith walking toward me. What did she want?

"Good morning, Anita," she said.

"Good morning, Edith."

"Donna is not coming in today."

133

"Oh, OK. Thanks," I said.

A few minutes later Donna called me. "Hi, Anita, I'll be home today if you need me."

"OK." I didn't ask if she was sick or anything. I really didn't care.

The phone rang. It was the shipping department. "Hi, Anita, is Donna in?"

"No, she will be in tomorrow," I said.

"I have some cartons here that belong to Donna and they can't stay here. What should I do with them?"

"How many cartons are there?"

"Ten cartons"

"OK, I guess bring them down."

I placed her infamous folders near her desk so when she came in they would be the first things she saw.

The next morning I walked into the office, and as always, Donna was already in and looking at the time on her computer.

"Good morning," I said.

"Good morning. I see my folders arrived," she said.

"They sure did. I wasn't sure where you wanted them."

"No, this is fine." She walked over to one of the opened boxes and pulled one out. "Check them out."

"Nice," I said.

"They do, right? Thanks. I worked very hard to get them done right." Donna said

I didn't say a word.

Donna went around showing the other departments her wonderful folders that no one would ever use.

When the invoice came in for the folders, Donna was called into the CFO's office.

"Anita, I will be back. I going to see Isaac" she said.

"OK," I said.

Isaac was the CFO of the company and has been with the company for fifteen years.

As she happily walked into Isaac's office, Edith was also sitting there. She was walking into an ambush.

"Come in Donna, and please close the door behind you."

As she sat down, she was saying to herself, *what the hell is going on? Am I getting fired?*

"Do you have these expensive folders you have created Donna?"

"Yes I do. I don't have one on me, but I can go and get one." Donna said

"Yes, you do that."

She came running into the office and grabbed her folder.

"Is everything OK?" I asked.

"Oh, yes the CFO wants to see one," Donna said.

"That's great."

She took off running.

Donna walked back into the CFO's office and closed the door behind her.

Twenty minutes later Donna returns to the office dazed and looking very pale.

She said, "You are not going to believe it, but you were right about Edith: she is a wolf in sheep's clothing."

"I guess you have experienced it, huh?"

"Oh, I sure did and I'm leaving early" Donna said.

The next day I was in the office before Donna. When she walked in I looked at my computer clock to see what time it is.

"Good morning Anita"

"Good morning Donna"

"I had such a headache after leaving Isaac's office"

"What happened?" I asked

"When I walked into his office Edith was already there. When I went to open the folder he cuts me off and asked me if I knew how much the folders cost?"

"How much were they?"

"I told him it cost fifty cents each"

"That's cheap" I said

"Yes that's what I thought and then he said to me that it cost them a total of ten fucking thousand dollars. Then he asked who authorized me to purchase the folders"? "

"He cursed?" I asked

"Yes"

"Did you get approval?" I asked

"Yes from Edith. I told him that Edith knew about it because I spoke to her. And he said that according to Edith that purchase was never authorized" Donna said

"What did Edith says?" I asked

"She said that we spoke about it but she never approved it. I would have never gone ahead with the order if she didn't approve it."

"So what happen?"

"Isaac said that everyone better use the folders in this fucking place. He was upset"

Donna took a couple of days off. She thought Edith was so wonderful. Edith would do that to everyone who worked for her and that's terrible.

When Donna came back on Monday she was different with me, kinder and more patient. Sometimes people needed to be grounded to learn a lesson. After the shock passes she will be back to normal.

As time passed on, things were going well. Donna only showed me some of the things that went on in production. I didn't ask her too many questions. I would call Denise, one of my best friends, and she would help me out. Denise and I worked together at Ivan Mandel and we always kept in touch.

It was summer time and I had on a white gauze shirt. I have a tattoo on my shoulder blade and it was visible through my shirt.

"Anita, is that a tattoo?" Donna asked

"Yes."

"I didn't know you have one. I think tattoos are for lowlifes."

"So you're calling me a lowlife?" I asked.

"No, but most people who have them are."

"That's not true, but it's your opinion. There are millions of low-lifes who do not have tattoos, and I'm sure we know many of them. Some are even working here."

She laughed. "Yes, I know."

How dare she say that to me? She should be careful because she had children who might get tattoos one day.

When Donna stepped away from her desk, I turned her computer off and then went to the bathroom. When I came back, she was turning her computer on.

"Anita, can you check your computer to see if it's on?" she asked.

I moved the mouse. "Yep, mine is on. Why?"

"I'm wondering why my computer keeps turning off."

I didn't say a thing. I kept doing my work. She hadn't learned her lesson with Edith. She would always be the bitch she was. And I would turn her computer off every time she turned into a one.

———

My phone kept ringing and ringing. Everyone was calling and complaining about Fema.

"Anita! Who are you talking to?" Donna asked.

I sighed, and my nose flared fire like a dragon's. I turned around and gave her the phone. "Here," I said. "Talk to them."

"This is Donna. Who's this?" she yelled into the phone.

"This is Edith, and why are you yelling? What is going on with you?"

Donna looked at me, and I gave her an "oh well" look. She turned pale. *Ha-ha, bitch. You wanted the phone, and you got it.*

"I didn't know it was you," she told Edith. "Sorry. I heard Fema's name."

"So it's OK to yell at her when she needs help?" Edith asked.

"No, and I apologize for that."

"Please send Anita up to see me," Edith said and then hung up the phone.

Donna turned to me. "Why didn't you tell me it was Edith?"

My nose flared again. "How could I when you were yelling while I was talking? You didn't even give me a chance to answer you."

"Well…"

"That's really unprofessional." I said.

"You're right. I'm sorry. Edith needs to see you."

"I'll be back," I said.

I didn't give her any eye contact as I walked away to see Edith. Damn bitch. What the hell was Donna's problem? I couldn't stand her. And what did Edith want? Maybe I was getting fired. Naw, it was only Monday. They usually fired people on Thursdays.

Eza was the director of Human Resources. It was really just a title because she had only one girl working for her, and that position had been filled several times since I'd started working there. I called her the grim reaper. If you saw Eza on your floor on a Thursday, you knew someone was getting the ax. They once fired two pregnant girls in one year. They fight dirty.

So I was safe that day, but I knew it was coming.

I walked into Edith's office. She said, "Sit down. What was going on with Donna?"

"She was upset because of the calls I was getting from everyone who needed help," I said.

"Really? Well, Fema is no longer with us. I had to let her go."

"Oh," I said.

"Do you want your job back?"

"No," I said.

"OK, but work with everyone until we find a solution."

"OK."

"Thank you."

Damn. Should I have taken the job back? A part of me thought I should have said yes, but entering orders was boring. The job was going nowhere. I hated production too, but I was going to learn everything I could.

—◊—

I stayed with Donna, and I asked many questions and learned everything about production. She wrote on my review that I was not focused, so I refused to sign it. It was not true. I was focused on the little bullshit work she gave me. After she gave me the review to sign, I was very cold toward her. She would never get it back.

—◊—

The company tried to develop a men's line to sell to stores like Kmart and Sears. They were trying to hit the urban market. The company needed help with the styles, UPC codes, and so on, and I was the one who would help.

My phone rang. "Hello," I said.

"Hi, Anita, it's Jennifer. Can you come up to see me?"

"Sure. I'll be right there."

I wondered what she wanted. I just walked away from my desk and didn't tell Donna anything. I went to Jennifer's office, put on my game face, and knocked on her door.

"Come in," she said, and I did. "I want to talk to you about a position. We acquired a company, and they need your help and expertise. Natasha is working with them now, but then she will be working for Donna."

Natasha was Margo's assistant. She has been with the company for three months.

"Oh, OK. So it's a switch," I said.

"Yes. Are you interested?"

"Sure." I could finally leave Donna.

"This is your time to shine," Jennifer said.

My time to shine for what? What the hell was she talking about, my time to shine?

"OK," I said.

"Come on. I'll walk with you. I have to go see Edith."

When we both stood up, we saw we had on the same shoes and slacks. Jennifer looked me up and down and said, "love the shoes."

"Thanks, love your shoes too."

One of the salesgirls walked into the hallway in front of us.

"Hi, Jennifer. Hi, Anita," she said.

I said, "Hi, Tamara."

"Hi Tamara" said Jennifer.

We all walked to the receptionist's area. I could see Jennifer eye-balling Tamara's outfit. I thought, *Damn, she's going to say something about it.*

Jennifer said, "Tamara, where did you get your outfit? At Daffy's?"

Wow, that was uncalled for, unprofessional and low class. How dare she belittle and degrade her staff? I could see why people hated her.

Tamara said, "Well, as a matter of fact, I did. My husband works there and I like my outfit."

Jennifer didn't say a word. She just looked at Tamara. Good for Tamara for saying something. I winked at her, and we smiled.

When Jennifer walked away, she almost tripped and fell.

I looked at Tamara and said, "You see? God don't like ugly."

"He sure doesn't. What the fuck was that all about? How dare she criticize what I wear? I come to work every day, and I work hard. What a miserable bitch."

"I liked what you said. She didn't know how to respond."

"I know, wasn't that great?"

"It sure was. I'm proud of you. Have a good day."

"You too," Tamara said.

—⚉—

The day I started in the new division, I went up to get some things I'd left at my desk. When I saw Natasha at my old desk with her eyes all watery, I knew that Donna had probably yelled at her.

"Hi, Natasha, how are you? Where is she?" I asked.

"That cow? Oh my God, how did you work with her? She's a fucking monster. Her eyes must be glued to the computer clock because every time I walk to my desk, she looks at me and then her clock and then back at me. How did you do it? She's not a nice woman."

"She did that to me too. Just make sure you get in on time. All I can tell you is do what's best for you."

"Don't tell anyone, but every morning when I walk in I say to her, 'Cow you doing?' instead of 'how you doing?' I hate her."

I said, "I understand, I'm here to get my things."

"Oh, here they are."

Donna walked in. "Oh my God! Chicky, how are you? How's it going there?" She was so phony. I was happy I was no longer working with her. I hated when she called me Chicky.

"Good, thanks. See you later."

"Nice seeing you again," Donna said.

I turned around to look at her, and I saw Natasha had a smirk on her face, as if to say, *This bitch is fake.* I nodded—*Yeah, I know.* Natasha smiled.

I went to lunch, and when I got back to my desk Natasha was talking to Margo in her office. I was sure she was venting.

My phone rang. It was Donna. She was probably looking for Natasha. I picked it up. "Hello, this is Anita."

"Hi, Anita. Is Natasha there?"

"Hi, Donna, and no, I have not seen Natasha. If I see her, I'll let her know you're looking for her."

"Oh, OK. Thanks."

I walked into Margo's office. "Excuse me. Natasha, Donna is looking for you."

"Oh my God, Margo, I hate her. I don't want to go back," Natasha said.

"Listen, you have to go back or quit," Margo said.

"I can't. I need a paycheck. OK, see you later." She walked out.

Margo was my new supervisor and the head of production for the new urban line. She reminded me of the witch in the Bugs Bunny Halloween cartoon that had pins flying out of her hair when she ran. She had that long chin; an awful mole near her nose; and curly, black, frizzy hair.

There was something about Margo that bothered me. I didn't know what it was, but it was something. She has been with the company for six months.

"Thanks for all your help," she said to me. "Natasha's great, but you know what you're doing, and we need that for the start-up. Between you and me, Edith was talking about you."

"Really? What did she say?" I asked.

"That you're not responsible, and you don't think outside the box. Listen, I know she's a bitch and a snake. She talks about everyone. I can't stand her. She's always yelling at me in meetings."

"She's a wolf in sheep's clothing," I said.

"She sure is. I've been looking to leave this place. I can't deal with Jennifer either. That fake-ass bitch."

"I know." I turned around and returned to my work.

———ɯ———

During the transition for the so-called urban line, a new member joined the team: Harry Lima, a little man with a big attitude. He came from an urban denim company. Natasha and I showed him the whole process of order entry.

Natasha and I were showing Harry how we entered the orders and the whole process. He was asking a lot of questions. Because I was not familiar with the division, I didn't say a word. Natasha was the one answering all the questions. I didn't like Harry. From his whole demeanor, I could tell he was a prick.

While I was working one day, Harry came to my desk.

"Hi, Anita. I have a question," he said.

"Yes," I said.

"What happened to the Sears order?"

"I think it shipped. I'm not sure, but I will ask Natasha."

"OK, let me know," he said.

I went upstairs to see Natasha, and of course Donna was there.

"Well, hello there Chicky," she said.

"Hello, Donna. Where's Natasha?" I asked.

"I don't know. She's like a jumping bean. She can't stay still."

I smiled. "Tell her to call me."

"OK Chicky, I will."

"Thanks."

When I got back, Natasha was just leaving Margo's office.

"Natasha, question: Harry was asking me about the Sears order. Do you know anything about it?"

"Yes, it wasn't shipped because of a UPC number. I spoke to Margo about it. She said she will take care of it." She said.

The next day Jennifer called me into her office. When I got there, Harry was sitting in one of the chairs. I knew something was up and not in a good way.

"Come in," Jennifer said.

I didn't say hello to Harry, and he didn't say anything to me either.

"What happened with the Sears order?" Jennifer asked.

"When Harry asked me about the order yesterday, I didn't know about it. I asked Natasha. She told me it hadn't shipped because there was an issue with one of the UPC numbers."

"No, you said it shipped," Harry said. "You made me look bad to Jennifer."

"I never told you it shipped because I just started in this division, and I wasn't aware of this order. So don't accuse me of saying something I didn't."

"Thank you, Anita. Harry, you can stay," Jennifer said.

He was a nitwit and a liar.

The following day Margo called in sick. It was Thursday. Mary, the receptionist from the thirty-fourth floor, was calling me.

"Hello," I said.

"Hi, Anita. Edith would like to see you in the conference room," she said.

"Is Eza around?" I asked.

"Yep."

"Girl, it's my turn."

"Oh, damn, Anita. I'm sorry," Mary said.

"It's OK. I've been here before. I've been in this war for a long time. It's nothing new in this business. Tell the wolf I'm coming up."

Before going to the conference room, I deleted all my spreadsheets and the contact names that I created. They could do their own research.

I walked into the conference room. Eza and Edith were sitting there with my folder.

I smiled and sat down. "Well, I guess it's my turn, huh?"

Edith said, "Anita, we have to let you go."

"You know, you never gave me a chance."

"Yeah, I know."

"Of course I didn't have a chance. You went up there and bad-mouthed me."

"No, I didn't."

I leaned real close to Edith, my teeth clenched together and my nose flaring. "Oh yes you did, because Margo told me. Anyway, why beat a dead horse?" I smiled.

She moved back and didn't say a word. She looked at Eza and asked, "Do you still need me here?"

"Anita?" Eza asked.

"What?"

"Do we need Edith to stay?"

I said, "No!"

"OK, Anita. Here are your checks," Eza said.

I snatched them. "Thanks for nothing. Good luck with her your new division." I hurried back to my desk, and I logged in and sent my last e-mail:

> Donna:
> Thanks for the wonderful review you gave me. It was all bullshit. I got fired because of you, and I know you didn't want me back.
> Thanks a lot.
> Anita

My phone rang. It was Margo.

"Hello," I said.

"Hi, Anita. I heard."

"You heard, or you already knew? Anyway, whatever." I hung up on her. She kept calling, but I didn't answer. I packed my stuff before Eza had a chance to come and watch over me.

When Eza walked over to me, I got up and said, "I'm done."

At the end it was all true: Natasha went back to work with Margo and Donna hired someone to assist her.

I heard later on that Donna went home early on the day I was fired, and then she moped around for two more days at work. After that she was back to normal.

Carmen, one of the cleaning ladies had a stroke in the office and died the following day. Six months later the urban division flopped, and the company closed it.

Twelve

FREELANCE

After 4 Apparel I was out of work for about two months. I was working with an agency called 24Seven. They are an employment agency for the fashion industry. The assignment was with a young, casual apparel and accessory company called Pastell. They manufactured jeans, T-shirts, jackets, hoodies, wallets, handbags, bracelets, and so on.

I would be freelancing with them for about three months, in the production department that handled all the denims. Their offices were on Thirty-Fourth Street, right in the center of the shopping world and near Macy's. Pastell occupied four floors, and there were lots of young people working there. The company employed about two hundred people.

It was my first freelance gig. I was not sure what to expect. Working freelance was not that bad because people couldn't boss you around. They gave me an assignment; I did it and then I went home. I worked from nine to five and had an hour for lunch. I felt no pressure, and things were calm for a change. I could probably get used to it.

Celeste was the girl to whom I reported. She was very pleasant, and her kindness was sincere. She wasn't fake, like most of the people in the industry. She didn't check her watch every time I walked in. I had a sign-in sheet, and at the end of the week she would sign it for me, and I would fax it over to the agency.

When Celeste showed me where I would be sitting, I went to put my purse on top of the shelf in the cubicle. There were mouse droppings on the shelves above me. Then I heard a scream.

"Ahh!"

Everyone ran to see what was going on, but I stayed at my desk. When Celeste came back, I asked, "What happened?"

"They caught a mouse on a glue trap," she said.

"Yuck."

"I know. They're running around all over this place."

"Yes, I know. There are mouse droppings on the shelf above me."

"Yuck. I'll contact HR and make sure they let the building-maintenance people know."

"That would be nice." I kept my purse on my lap all day as I worked. I was afraid I would bring a mouse home with me in my purse if I put it down.

—⚯—

My assignment at Pastell was almost over, and I was hoping they would keep me. Three days before my last day, I got a call for an interview for a job. I went but found no luck there.

On my last day, Celeste said, "Thank you so much, Anita. You were so helpful. Can you stay for three more weeks?"

"Sure!" I said.

"Wow, that's great. Thank you."

"Thank you."

I was happy that I had three more weeks to find a job.

Things were going well. Friday was ice cream day. They had the works: several flavors, nuts, cones, sprinkles, whipped cream, and cherries. Who would want to leave?

"Anita, are you coming with up for some ice cream?" Celeste asked me one Friday.

"Sure."

There were lots of employees already there. While Celeste and I were on line, the office manager came up to me and asked with an attitude, "Who are you?"

"I'm a freelancer here," I said.

"And who invited you?"

Before I could answer, Celeste said, "Who are you? And why are you asking her why she's here? She works with me, and I invited her. Do you have a problem with that?"

"Oh, I didn't know," the office manager said.

"Well, now you know."

The woman walked away mad.

"How dare she talk to you like that? I can't stand her. I just wanted to punch her out," Celeste said.

We both smiled.

"I see why, and thank you" I said.

"Your welcome. One day she tried to bully me, and I wasn't having it. I told her to fuck off, and now she's nice to me because she knows I won't take her shit."

We both laughed.

"Wow, next week is your last week. Did you find a job?" Celeste asked.

"Yes, I did. It's a fabric company. I start next week."

"Wow, that's great. Too bad we can't hire you permanently."

"I know it would have been wonderful. I really like it here," I said.

"Here's my card. Call me if you ever need a reference."

"I will. Thanks."

Thirteen

SHEM FABRICS

Shem Fabrics had been in business for more than forty years, selling to clients like Barneys, Saks, Brooks Brothers, and many high-end companies. They also specialized in custom, fitted men's dress shirts, and their client list was huge: there were hundreds from Wall Street alone.

I was hired as a sales assistant. I would be working for two sales reps: Morris and Jeff.

Morris had been with the company for seven years. Two years earlier he had been promoted to sales manager. He was very high maintenance and had trouble keeping an assistant

Jeff had been with the company for about two years. He was easygoing and did most of his own work.

Sophie had been with the company for ten years as the HR department's pet. She traveled to New York if she had to, but she was based out of New Jersey. She had long, thin, curly hair and wore an awful rust-colored eye shadow that made her look like a corpse.

On Monday morning I was ready for whatever. I always stayed positive wherever I went. There were three other girls who were sales assistants too: Gina, Kathy, and Angela. They seemed nice. All of us sat together in one area except for Angela. She sat with the sales reps, who all sat in cubicles. There was not a lot of room. Angela did a lot of traveling, so we hardly saw her.

Kathy and Gina each sat in a cubicle with shelves. My desk was just in a corner, and that was that. I was behind Gina, and Kathy was on my right. She would roll her chair if she needed me or if we all wanted to chat. Angela was in a cubicle opposite Gina's.

I met everyone in the office.

Kathy was a single mom of two. She had been with the company for two years. She was Eric's assistant.

Gina was married and had been with the company for five years. She was the vice president's assistant. His name was Michael. She loved working for him because he gave her huge raises and bonuses every year.

Michael had been with the company for twelve years. He made a lot of money, and he lived on Central Park West, overlooking the park.

Angela had been with the company for seven years. She was a newlywed.

One morning while I was getting some coffee in the kitchen, Gina and Kathy walked in. They both said good morning.

"Good morning, ladies," I said.

Gina said, "We have something to tell you."

"Yes we do," Kathy said.

"OK. What is it?" Now what were they going to tell me?

Kathy made sure there was no one around and then she said, "OK, tell her."

"You are the fifth girl in this position in a year and a half," Gina said.

My heart sank. "Really? Damn." I looked at Kathy.

"Yup."

"Morris is the problem, right?" I asked.

Gina looked at Kathy and then at me. "How did you know?"

"I'm not a fool. I spotted him from a mile away. Plus if there were four assistants in a year and a half, he is definitely a problem."

Kathy said, "We're sorry. We had to tell you because we really like you."

Gina said, "We really do."

I smiled. "Thanks. I really appreciate that you told me. I like you guys too."

Kathy said, "We thought you should know."

"Thanks again."

I sighed all the way home, all I could think about was how the hell I had gotten a job that had that kind of history. But how could I have known? I was the fifth person in the position in a year and a half. Wow. I couldn't believe it was happening to me again. I felt like a walking target.

As the days passed, I tried to learn how "the fax" worked, and it was overwhelming. The fax was a bunch of questions and answers in a Word document that was on the server for everyone to add their comments. Whoever had it last would fax it over to the factories in Italy and China. It was about ten pages of questions and answers. When I read it, it made me nauseous. I had to make sure Jeff and Morris, especially Morris, answered the questions addressed to them. You would think they would e-mail each other individually. I took a deep breath and kept it moving. I was there to do the job to the best of my ability.

Things were OK. The busy season was coming, and so were the holidays. Working with Morris was very stressful, and most of his clients were also high maintenance. There was so much work, I really couldn't catch up. Our factories were in Italy and China, so we had to make sure we answered the questions on the fax that were sent from them at the end of the day. Once you got a hold of the fax, you'd better answer all the questions before someone else got it. If you lost your turn, you had to wait until the others were finished, and it could be a while.

There was always something Morris wanted to add to the fax just when I had my coat on to go home. Every night as I was walking out the door, I had to pass his office. I always prayed he wouldn't see me and call me in.

As I passed Morris's door one day, he said, "Good night."

"Good night," I said, and then I walked out as fast as I could.

The next day I was not that lucky. As I was packing my stuff and getting ready to go home, he called me. "Anita, did you go over the fax?"

"Yes, I did, and I answered the questions."

"Oh, OK. Are you leaving?"

"Yes. Why?"

"I want to go over some of the questions on the fax."

"OK. I'll be right in." Shit, I was so ready to leave; it was 5:20 p.m., and he knew I left at 5:30.

I walked into Morris's office, and we got right to it. We went over two questions because I had answered everything else, as he wanted me to.

"You did well on the answers," he said. "I thought there were more questions. Thanks. Have a good night."

It was good because it only took ten minutes. So I was leaving on time.

"OK, good night," I said.

I got up to leave, and he said, "Oh, and by the way, Jeff and I are leaving for China in a few weeks. So tomorrow let's go over some things."

"OK."

"Good night, and thanks for your help."

"You're welcome. Good night." I walked out of there so fast, you'd have thought the place was on fire.

All I could do was what Jeff and Morris asked of me. They were leaving for China for two weeks, and I was left in the office to help their clients. I was a bit nervous because it was all new to me. Gina was assigned to help me with Morris' clients.

On the day they arrived in China, Morris was already calling the office, and there was a twelve-hour time difference. He sent me an e-mail with a millions things he wanted me to do at the office. I had to do reports for certain customers to track their orders and spreadsheets. Jeff took care of all of his clients; he didn't have much for me to do.

Morris called every day to see how the faxes were going. I didn't do much with the China fax because they were there and were taking care of everything. I took care of the customers calling the office and the Italian factories.

One day I was working on a report with orders and delivery dates for Morris' clients. Gina was talking with him about some orders that had come from China.

"Anita, it's your turn," Gina said.

I sighed and then picked up the phone. "Hello."

"Hey, Anita, did you do the spreadsheet for Brooks Brothers?" Morris asked.

"Yes," I said.

"How about Bloomingdale's?"

"Yes."

"Macy's, Saks, and Barneys?"

"Yes, yes, and yes."

"OK, thanks. Good-bye," Morris said.

"Good-bye." I hung up.

The next morning, as soon as I sat down and took a sip of my coffee, the phone rang.

"Gina, Morris is on line one for you," I heard the receptionist say.

I took my coffee and went into the kitchen. Kathy followed me and said, "It's nine at night there. I'm sure he couldn't wait to call."

We both giggled and I said, "Yeah, I know. It's like he smells us in the office."

Kathy laughed so hard, she snorted, and that made us laugh more until Gina walked in, looked at me, and said, "It's your turn."

I looked at Kathy. "Fun's over."

"Yeah, I know. Good luck."

"Thanks."

I took a long sip of my coffee and a deep breath, and I answered the phone.

"Good morning."

"Good morning. Everything OK?" Morris asked.

"Yes, everything is good."

"OK, talk to you later."

He called again and talked with Gina for a while. Afterward she turned to me and said, "You're it again."

"Damn. I just spoke to him," I said. We laughed as I picked up the phone. "Hello."

"Can you fax the spreadsheet for Brooks Brothers over to me?" Morris asked.

"Sure," I said.

"OK, I'll call you back."

About twenty minutes later, he called again. "Anita, I don't see the latest orders."

"You never gave me the latest orders. I added everything you gave me," I said.

"There was an order for Barneys for style BY550 in gray flannel. Did you enter it? I don't see it. I only see BY551 black wool."

"There's no order for Barneys in that style, only BY551 black wool."

His voice went up a bit. "Are you sure? I know I gave them to you."

Then my voice got higher. "No! You gave me the order for BY551 black wool, and it's in your handwriting."

"No I wrote BY550," Morris said.

"No you didn't, check the order."

"All right, sorry," Morris said.

The girls looked at me when I hung up the phone.

"Asshole," I said.

Gina and Kathy curiously rolled their chairs over to me.

"What happened?" Gina asked.

"There's some order he claims he gave me and he didn't. I took all the orders that were on his desk, and it wasn't there," I said.

Kathy said, "Good for you. None of his assistants ever yelled at him."

"Well, there's a new sheriff in town," I said.

We all laughed.

"I'm sorry, but I am not going to allow anyone to yell at me. If he doesn't like it, he can fire me. I've been fired from better places."

That Friday a memo went out that Sophie was coming to work in New York for a while. No one knew why. All the girls were pissed. The receptionist, Sybil, couldn't stand Sophie's guts. They had exchanged words several times regarding Sybil's lateness.

Sybil had been with the company for almost two years. She was a single mom in her early twenties.

Gina said, "You know she's coming here to spy on us."

Sybil banged her fist on her desk. "I can't believe she's coming here. I can't stand her."

"I can't stand her either," Gina said.

Kathy smirked. "And where is she going to sit? On my lap?"

I didn't say anything because I had met Sophie only one time. Whether she was in the office or not, my work ethic would be the same.

The holidays arrived, and things were going OK. For Christmas I got a $2,000 bonus. I was so surprised; I had not been expecting anything. I was grateful, especially since I had been there for only a few months. I could imagine what the bonuses were after several years.

The following week there were several meetings. Something was going on. When Kathy and I came back from lunch one day, we saw Gina crying. Gina was a drama queen as it was, so it could have been anything.

"What's the matter?" Kathy asked her.

"Michael was fired," Gina said.

"Wow, when?"

"Just now. What am I going to do? First it was my divorce, and now this? Oh my God, what am I going to do?"

Kathy and I looked at each other. Gina went into the bathroom.

Kathy said, "Oh my God, she's such a drama queen. And now she's going to bitch about this all day long. Don't you hear her? She goes on and on about the same thing. This is going to drive me crazy."

"Yes, I do, and sometimes I just want to say, 'Shut up!' But what are you going do?"

We both laughed.

I saw Gina coming back. "Here she comes."

"How are you doing?" Kathy asked.

"I'm OK, I guess," said Gina.

I said, "Listen, things get better as time passes."

"Yeah, I know, but what I am going to do? I think I'm going to leave early." She took her purse and walked out.

—⟋⟍—

Sophie arrived at the New York office. She settled in one of the small showrooms and made it into her own little office. She was now the office manager, and the girls were not happy at all. As for me, it really didn't matter because I didn't have any problem with her yet.

As I walked toward my desk, Kathy and Gina motioned me to come to the kitchen. What now?

"What happened?" I asked.

"Where is she?" Gina asked.

"Who?," I asked.

"Sophie," said Kathy.

"She's in her office."

"I heard that she asked for that showroom as an office so she can see when we all come in" Gina said.

"I don't like people watching me" Kathy said.

I didn't say anything; I just listened. Something about Sophie bothered me, but I wasn't sure what it was. At some point everyone shows who they really are.

Several months passed, and everything was going good.

We heard several people talking, and we heard a baby. Kathy rolled her chair over and looked at Gina and me. "Who's that?" she asked.

Gina said, "Let me find out."

It was a former employee, Holly, who had come by with her baby and husband. Holly had worked at the company for several years as Eric's assistant. She walked around the office showing everyone her baby. I didn't meet her, but I did see her from a distance. She had left two years earlier because she wanted to be a stay-at-home mom.

Eric was the president of the company. He had been there for twenty-five years.

Several weeks later Morris called me into his office. "Close the door, and come sit down," he said.

I knew something was up. Before I sat down I said, "You're firing me?"

He tilted his head and squinted his eyes. "Yes."

"Why?"

"There were too many reports you never followed up on, and the customers were upset."

"I did exactly what you wanted, so I don't understand." I pressed my lips tightly together.

"Yes, I know, and I'm sorry." He handed me a check.

"Yeah, sure you are." I took the check and walked out. I walked to my desk to gather my stuff, and then I went over to Kathy and Gina.

"Hey," I said.

They both turned around.

"What's up?" Gina asked.

"I was let go."

Kathy's eyes watered. "What?"

"Yep."

Gina said, "What did he say?"

"He mumbled about some reports, but I know it's something else."

"I'm so sorry," Gina said.

"It's just a day in my life."

We hugged, and I walked out. I sat on the steps of St. Patrick's Cathedral for a while to collect my thoughts. *Here I go again. God help me.*

A few days later, I received an e-mail from Morris saying if I ever needed a reference to please contact him and that he was sorry.

As soon as I read the e-mail, my phone rang. It was Kathy.

"Hey, Anita, how are you?" she asked.

"I'm OK. I just received an e-mail from Morris saying he'll give me a reference if I need one," I said.

"Well, do you?"

"Nah."

"I have something else to tell you."

"What?"

"Holly is working here."

"Who?" I asked.

"Holly. Remember, she came to the office with her husband and baby?"

"Yeah."

"Her," Kathy said.

"Oh shit, really? That's why they fired me? To hire her?"

"Yep. I'm sorry."

"Please, girl, don't be. It's part of my life. Well, I never would have met you, right?"

"Yeah, you're right," she said.

"Thanks for telling me," I said.

"Sure, take care."

"Yeah, you too."

A few minutes later, Gina called me.

"Hey, Anita, how are you?" she asked.

"Hi, Gina. I'm OK."

"Listen, Morris asked me if I'd spoken to you."

"Why does he care?" I asked.

"He feels bad for letting you go."

"What for? I would have respected him if he'd told me the truth—that they were hiring Holly back."

"Yeah, I know. What should I tell him?" she asked.

"Tell him what I told you."

Everything comes out in the end, but he didn't have the balls to tell me the truth.

There I was, looking for another job, and I needed to find one fast. But it was not fast enough. It took two years, and I was on my last unemployment check. I couldn't afford to buy fabric for my handbags, but I kept on sketching.

I checked my e-mail everyday, all day. Finally a company I had sent my resume asked that I call for an interview. I retired the red suit, so I can go more casual. Black slacks and a black button down shirt.

Fourteen

ROLL-ON

Roll-On was a luggage company in business for fifteen years. They were located on Thirty-Third and Fifth Avenue.

I called about the interview. "Hi, can I speak to Frank?"

"Speaking."

"Hi, I'm Anita."

"Yes, thank you for calling. You said you have some experience with QuickBooks?" Frank asked.

"Yes, I've worked with QuickBooks, but it was several years ago. Where do you ship from?"

"California."

"Is it a public warehouse or your own?"

"Public," he said.

"How many people work in the office, and how many enter orders?"

"Who's doing the interview, you or me?"

I laughed. He was kind of rude. I forgot that it was just a data-entry position not a managerial position.

"When can you come in?" Frank asked.

"I can come today around eleven thirty."

"That's perfect. We're on Eighteen West and Thirty-Third Street, on the third floor."

"OK, see you soon."

Though the salary was very, very low, I needed a job, and I needed it right away.

The office was nothing fancy: a small showroom, slat walls, and bags hanging everywhere. They sold regular and sports-team luggage.

"Hi," I said to the receptionist. "I'm here to see Frank."

"Sure. Your name?"

"Anita Martini."

He picked up his phone. "Frank, Anita Martini is here to see you." He hung up and said to me, "He'll be right out."

"Thank you," I said.

A few seconds later, Frank walked over to me. We shook hands.

"Hi, Anita, I'm Frank," he said.

"Hello."

Frank Pebbles was very garmento, with his straight-leg jeans, cowboy boots, and open shirt. He also wore turquoise rings and a bracelet. He reminded me of Donny from Donny & Co. but with a mullet.

During the interview, Frank asked me several questions.

"So, Anita, if you were on a field with a brick wall in front of you, and it was about twenty feet high and miles across on each side, how would you get to the other side?"

"OK, let me get this straight: how would I get to the other side of a twenty-foot-high brick wall that is miles wide? I would dig a hole to the other side."

"With what will you dig the hole?" Frank asked.

I showed him both of my hands. "With these."

"I just want to know where you are."

"Yes, I know."

He laughed. "You know, this is the most aggressive interview I have ever conducted."

"And the one you will always remember," I said.

"I sure will. OK, let's say you're the only one in the office, and someone calls and says their shipment never arrived. What are you going to do?"

"First I would find out how it was shipped. If I couldn't find out how it was shipped, I would call the warehouse to see what was going on, especially since they're three hours behind us."

"OK. If you are the only one in the office, and the fire alarm rings, what will you do?"

What was going on? I'm not a psycho, why is he psychoanalyzing me. "I would make sure I'm the only one in the office, and then I would take the stairs to the lobby and ask security what's going on."

"OK, one more thing. Can you write down what you did over the weekend?"

"Sure."

What the hell? Now he wanted to know what I did on weekends. I felt like I was in school.

"I want to see how you write," Frank said.

"OK."

Then the other owner came into the office. "Hi," he said. "My name is Tom. I'm the better half."

I smiled and said, "Hi, I'm Anita."

He nodded and smiled and kept on reading. He was going through my résumé.

"With this résumé why has no one called you?"

"I don't know. You tell me."

"OK, thank you," he said and then walked away.

Frank said, "Come, let's go to the front desk. I want to test you on QuickBooks. OK?"

"OK."

"Would you like some water?" he asked.

"Yes, please."

When we got to the front desk, he said, "Sit here. I want you to find the inventory for style AVD1258 and I want you to run a sales report for that very same style. Do well please."

"I'll try, but I haven't worked on QuickBooks in a long time," I said.

"Do your best."

"I always do." I should have told him, "Do your best on the salary because it sucks."

I sat down, and a girl approached me. "Hi, I'm Mary. Frank wants me to show you how to run a report."

"OK. Thanks."

Then someone else came over. "Hi, can you please fix this spreadsheet and make the changes that are in red and print it?"

"OK, no problem." It took me a few minutes to complete.

Frank came to the front desk and walked me into the showroom. "Thank you for coming in. We'll make a decision, and I will let you know."

"Thank you."

We shook hands, and I walked out.

After a few calls back and forth with Frank, he offered me the job. I would be entering e-commerce orders and handling customer service.

Roll-On's offices were right across the street from the Empire State Building. I'd always loved working in that area because of all the shopping I could do. I sat in the back office with three other girls. Some girls can be catty and jealous. There were only a few good and decent women in this business.

Mary had been with the company for six years. She handled the larger orders and freight.

Vicky had been with the company for only a year. She handled the credit with the bank and customer service.

Elizabeth came in once a week; the others days she worked from home. She has been with the company for four years and handles EDI and invoicing.

Leslie was the designer. She had been with the company for seven years. Leslie and John shared an office.

The girls were OK, and we got along. Maybe because I was older than they were. Actually I was the oldest employee there besides the owners, and they were close to sixty. I wasn't near that age.

There were times I was asked to file, and I was OK with it. I wasn't above filing. I did my job from nine to five, and then I went home.

—ɱ—

One day I heard someone yelling, "What the fuck is wrong with you? Are you an idiot?"

"Vicky," I said.

She turned around. "Yeah?"

"Who's that yelling?"

She smiled. "That's Frank yelling at Brian or John."

"Damn, he sounds like my old boss."

Then I heard him say, "This is my company, not yours. You do what I tell you or you can leave."

I didn't like that. How did I get to be working for more nitwits? Sigh. I felt uneasy in the pit of my stomach when I heard Frank yelling and what he was saying. If he yelled at them like that, I was sure he would yell at me like that too.

Damn. Would I ever work for a company that had nice people? I would win the lottery before I worked for nice bosses. It was people with titles who acted that way because they signed the paychecks. But that didn't mean they could abuse you. There were ways of saying things without being disrespectful.

John had worked for Roll-On for seven years. He was a sales rep for the house accounts.

Brian had been with the company for eight months. He was also a house sales rep. He sat at the front desk. There was no room for him to sit anywhere else.

I knew that one day Frank would yell at me. And I knew I would not be working there long because of the yelling that was going on. I was more afraid of what I would do. One day I was going to snap! Frank's yelling was unprofessional and unnecessary; he could get his point across in another way. I prayed to God every day that I wouldn't have to go out of character. I needed to change what I did. Entering orders and shipping was not for me anymore. I did it for the clothing allowance.

—⁕—

One day I was asking a customer how many pieces she had received in an order, and Tom was listening to what I was saying. I sat in front of his office.

"Anita who are you talking to?" he asked, coming out to my desk.

I stayed calm even though he was yelling, and I was on the phone. "Ma'am, please hold," I said and then I answered Tom. "It's Blue Ridge. She was shipped style 20ATH, one piece, to her store and her sister store, and she's wondering where the other two pieces are."

"She has to order three pieces," Tom said.

I had the customer on hold. "She did order three but received only one, and she's asking for her other two pieces."

"You tell her she has to take all three."

"But I just told you she already received only one." There were some styles that were shipped three in a box, and customers had to order them in threes.

"Well, you tell her she has to take all three," Tom said again.

"But she already has one that was shipped to her."

"I don't give a shit. You tell her she has to take three."

I took a deep breath. I looked at the other girls, and they shook their heads. I knew Tom was wrong, and I already knew what the customer was going to say.

"Hi, ma'am," I said, going back to the call. "You have to take the three pieces."

"But why should I when you already shipped me one piece?" she asked.

"I know, but my boss said you have to take the three pieces because we ship in sets of three."

"Well, cancel my order and my sister company's orders too. Also, let me talk to your boss."

"Hold on." I put the call on hold and said, "Tom, she wants to talk to you."

"I'm not talking to her. I didn't tell you I wanted to talk to her," he said.

"But she's going to cancel her orders because she already received the one piece, and she wants the other two."

"I don't give a shit. You tell her she has to take them."

"Why don't you talk to her?"

While walking away Tom said, "No, I'm not talking to her."

"Fine," I said. What a nitwit. If you have a rule, stand by it, and talk to the customer.

"Ma'am? Sorry about that. I will ship the other two pieces to you and your sister store."

"Thank you," she said.

I couldn't believe he'd had me tell her that. Sigh. I wouldn't be staying there long. I had lost respect for Tom. What a douche.

I was there again. I'd thought working for women was bad, but damn. It's people. Tom had a belittling way of talking to us. One day someone was going to punch him in his big mouth; maybe it would be me.

Tom Slurps and Frank Pebbles had been partners for almost ten years. His office was to the right of where I sat. His last name fit him perfectly because he would make slurping noises when drinking coffee and "ah" noises after he finished. It was so annoying. I just wanted to clobber him. And when he was sick, we would hear his disgusting cough.

Things were going OK, but I continued to search for another job. Things at Roll-On started to get busy. The holidays were coming, and Christmas was a busy time. The company asked that we not take vacations from Thanksgiving through the New Year.

One day Tom said, "Anita, I need you to work on the weekends during the holidays, to bring in and enter the orders."

"You want me to come here?" I asked.

"No, you can work from home."

"Am I getting paid for it?"

"No," he said.

"No? Why not?"

"Why not? It's part of the job."

"No, it's not."

"Yes, it is. It's the law."

"No, it's not," I said. He swore he knew everything.

"You will get paid for it at the end of the year."

"Then you should have said that first," I said. *Nitwit.*

I didn't say anything else. That was not the law, and no one had said to me during the interview that I would have to work on weekends. So I would wait to see what kind of bonus I would get at the end of the year. I was not expecting much because the company is cheap.

I worked from home every weekend in the month of December. When I got my bonus, it was $1,000; after taxes it was about $700. It was better than nothing, but they could have done better.

One day I heard Brian say to John, "You'd better stop talking shit about me, or I'll punch your lights out."

I didn't hear anything from John. They were always arguing with each other. John and Brian did not get along.

Brian walked to the back office. "Can you believe this lazy ass? He watches TV on his laptop while everyone else is working."

Mary said, "Oh that's nothing new."

I said, "Oh, I'm at the right company. All play and no work."

Vicky said, "Yeah, for them, but not for us in the back office."

Mary said, "You can say that again."

We all laughed.

The next day Frank was on a rampage about something. He was yelling at Leslie about the catalog. "You said you will take care of it and you haven't. Why?"

Leslie said, "Because you have me doing something else."

"I need you to take care of it now. This is my company, not yours."

I heard him walk away. The floors were wood, so everyone heard someone coming.

Leslie and Brian shared an office. She walked to the back, with her eyes red and watery, to make a copy.

"I'm going to lunch." She walked out without looking at us.

"Is he always like this?" I asked.

"Yeah, when he's got a bug up his ass. He's made me cry too," Mary said.

"That's not good," I said.

"No it's not," Vicky said.

—◠◠◠—

One morning we were all in the office, working, when the police went into Tom's office and closed the door. We all looked at each other as if to say, *What is going on?* After fifteen minutes they walked out.

Frank walked into the office and said, "Vicky, come with me please."

We all looked at each other.

When Vicky came back, she looked like a dragon with smoke coming out of her nose. She was pissed. She looked at us and said, "Yo, what the fuck?" Her eyes were watery. "They asked me if I know a Rhonda Williams. I said no. Then Tom said, 'Are you sure?' Then Frank said, 'You know, we have a picture of what she looks like.' Then they said I can work out something with them."

"Work what out?" I asked.

"A fucking payment plan. Why? Because I'm black? I'm so hurt by this. I'm not paying for shit."

"Damn, that's fucked up." I said.

Mary was going to say something when Frank walked in and said, "Anita, can we see you?"

I looked at the girls. When I walked into Frank's office, he closed the door. I sat, and then Tom asked, "Do you know a Rhonda Williams?"

"No," I said.

"So you don't know Rhonda Williams?"

"No."

"OK. Thank you."

Then they called in Mary.

The questions they asked Vicky were not the same ones they asked Mary and I. Vicky's questions were more like, "We know you did it, so fess up." They were racist.

Then Frank came out again. "Vicky, can we see you again?"

We all looked at each other again. I thought, *Damn, they probably think it was her.*

Mary said, "What do you think it is?"

"I think someone stole money or something."

"Why do you say that?"

"Because he told Vicky they have this girl on the bank's surveillance camera, so it has to be that."

"You're right. Do you think Vicky did it?"

"No way. Do you?"

Mary paused and then said, "I don't think so."

From what I knew about Vicky, I doubted she'd had anything to do with it. Fifteen minutes later she came back looking steamed.

I said, "What happened?"

"They asked me if I'm willing to take a lie-detector test and to sign Tom's name. I signed Tom's name, but I said no to the lie detector."

"What?"

Frank came into the office. "Anita, can you come in, please?"

Then it was Mary's turn.

Frank and Tom asked us the same questions. I noticed they never called in Brian, John or Leslie. Why? Because they were white too. I would have bet the farm on it. They could have done it.

Vicky said, "I'm going to the bathroom." She grabbed her cell phone and walked out the door.

I went after her. "What's going on?"

She started to cry. "They are not asking me if I knew. They're telling me, as if I had something to do with it. I called my uncle. He's a district attorney in Jersey City."

"Good."

"He told me not to sign anything," Vicky said.

"Good. Listen to him."

"I have to call him again."

"OK, I'll see you in the office," I said.

When Vicky came back, her eyes were puffy from crying. "I'm going out to lunch," she said and then grabbed her purse and left the office.

I lost all the respect for the company because of what they did to Vicky. I had to find another job and fast.

Tom and Frank had a belittling way of talking to her. It bothered me because I had been through that before and had been fired as a result of it too. I'd rather get fired than take the verbal abuse. One day Frank walked into the back office and asked, "Vicky, who told you not to ship the order?"

"Mary said not to ship it," Vicky said.

"Mary doesn't own the company. I do."

"I know, but—"

He cut her off. "You do what I tell you."

"It feels like you guys treat me differently," she said.

"Well, if you don't like it you can leave."

I felt like he was talking to me, and he really was because it was meant for all of us.

Wow, that was not right. That was the shit that would happen to me, and I would be prepared for that, but to see it done to Vicky hurt me. It shouldn't have happened, but it did and always to the underdogs. But we fight back. Some people can underestimate our intelligence and then try to test it.

Vicky had a lot of learning to do. She would get it. The next day she e-mailed Frank and told him she would be coming in late. He e-mailed her back and said not to come back.

We had a code to get into the office, and every day the company changed it. So every day we would learn the code for the day, and the next day was the same thing. They were probably thinking Vicky would show up even though they had told her not to come back.

—◊—

Frank walked to the back. "Hi, ladies. Everything OK?" he asked. We all nodded.

"Anita, how many orders do we have today?"

"We got about twenty-five." I pointed to his shoes and asked, "Hey, are those Donny & Co.?"

He looked surprised and said, "Yes, how do you know?"

"Size eleven, right?"

"Damn, you're good. But how do you know?"

I happened to have the same shoes on but for women. "See?" I said, and I showed him my shoes.

"We have the same style," Frank said.

"I also used to work for Donny & Co."

"Really? I love his shoes. I always wanted to work for him."

I smiled and left it at that. I hoped he wouldn't be looking for a discount because even if I could give him one, I wouldn't. Ever!

———✺———

I heard Frank yelling again. It was like I was back at Essex. Ira and Frank were probably cousins.

"I told you to have the report ready," Frank said.

"I'm not done yet," Brian said.

"But you said the report was ready."

"I'm not going to babysit you. Just get it done."

Frank walked to the back office and said, "Good night, ladies."

Mary and I said good night. I thought he was bipolar. One minute he was yelling, and the next minute he was acting like nothing had ever happened. Though it was a small office, and I couldn't hide, I tried not to talk to Frank much.

There were a lot of people in the building who didn't like him. He complained to the building management every time someone hammered. He would call them and tell them the noise needed to stop when it was one of our neighbors renovating a showroom. One of the neighbors came and argued with him. When I saw the neighbor on the elevator later, he said, "Your boss, Frank, is a prick."

I said, "Yes, I know that."

———✺———

After ten months Frank called me into his office. Tom was also there. "Yes?" I asked.

Tom asked, "How long does it take you to enter, say, thirty orders?"

"I don't know. Let me count how many orders I have, and I'll get back to you," I said. I left the office, went to my desk, and went back. "I happen to have thirty orders."

Frank said, "OK. Start now, and let us know when you finish."

It was bullshit. Tom had asked Mary why was I slow. I didn't understand what they wanted from me. After an hour I went back.

"OK, I'm done."

Tom looked at me like I was lying. He had his lips pressed tightly together. I just looked at him. My nose was starting to flare.

Frank said, "OK. What else are you doing?"

"I'm answering e-mails, sending tracking, and answeing customer-service calls."

"What kinds of calls?"

"Calls about invoices, double shipments, and tracking information. Every call is different," I said.

"OK. Tomorrow, about nine fifteen, we'll test you again," Frank said.

"Yeah, sure."

"OK. Thanks."

No wonder no one stayed there. Mary told me one day that there a girl had been working there for a few weeks. When Frank yelled at her, she went to her desk for her purse and told him she wasn't coming back. Another girl went to use the bathroom during the interview and never came back.

Frank's comments bothered me all night. When I got in the next morning, I walked into his office.

"Got a minute?" I asked.

"Yeah, sure. What's up, Anita?"

"I've been here for ten months, and you want to test me now?"

"Why are you getting defensive?" Frank asked.

"I'm not getting defensive," I said.

"Yes, you are."

"I'm not getting defensive, Frank, I'm just asking. The day I get defensive, you will know."

"Tom and I are restructuring the company."

"What do you mean?"

"We want to change things around."

"OK."

"Let me know when you're ready, so I can test you again."

"Let me check how many orders I have."

"OK."

I walked out, went to my desk, and came back. "I have sixteen orders."

"OK. Start now."

I left to enter the orders, and thirty-five minutes later I came back and said, "I'm done."

He nodded and said, "OK. Thanks."

They just wanted to make sure I was not lying. I have never in all my years been tested on how fast or slow I worked as long as it was getting done.

—⚹—

While I was entering orders, Tom yelled, "How do you spell recipient?"

I said, "R-e-c-i-p-i-e-n t."

He yelled again, "Can someone tell me how to spell recipient?"

I yelled back, "I just did."

"That is not right."

We all looked at each other. Then I said, "Can someone tell Tom how to spell recipient?"

Mary said, "R-e-c-i-p-i-e-n-t."

"OK. Thanks," Tom said.

I turned to the girls. "You see what I mean?"

They shook their heads in understanding. If Mary weren't Spanish, I would think it was racial, but it was personal.

—⟋⟍—

Brian gave his two weeks' notice; he was leaving the company. He handled warranties and RA, which is short for "return authorization." The company gave a five-year warranty on all of their merchandise. If a bag was damaged, we shipped the customer another bag at no charge with proof of damage.

Now that Brian was leaving, the company decided to give the RA's and Warranties to me on top of all the other stuff I had to do.

Brian said to Tom in front of me, "Hey, Tom, you know Anita has a lot on her plate. It should go to John, he was not that busy."

His words fell on death ears. He even told Frank, but Frank didn't listen either. That was that; it was now my responsibility. It should have gone to John because he was a salesperson, and he knew the product better than I did. Plus he had a lot of time on his hands.

When Brian left Frank said, "Anita, you will be all right with the warranties. You'll know all the styles within a few weeks."

Frank had been in business for fifteen years, and he was always asking Mary which style was which. And I'm suppose to know all the styles in a few weeks. He's out of his mind.

—⟋⟍—

I said to Tom, "You know, I have a lot to do, and I'm not sure when I'll be able to get to the warranties."

"You'll do it. You're fast," he said.

"Who said I'm fast?"

"You can enter thirty orders in an hour."

"But that has nothing to do with the warranties." I was so overwhelmed, and they didn't care. It was time to go.

I couldn't believe they knew John was not busy, yet they wanted to pile more shit on my plate. They were taking advantage of me.

Frank said, "Anita, you can do the warranties on Tuesdays and Thursdays."

"OK." That was all I said because we would have gotten into it, and I would have lost. I was fighting a losing battle. I couldn't stand working there anymore. I felt like crying.

Every morning when I walked into the office, I made the sign of the cross to help me through the new day. Every Monday I wore black to mourn my weekends.

That morning as I was approaching the building I saw a man lying dead on the ground. The police arrived immediately. We heard later on that it was an employee who shot his boss three times because he fired him. It was all over the news and newspaper. I used to see him on the elevator and he looked arrogant. He should have beat him up, but not kill him. I don't condone, but I understand. People can push you and you can snap at any minute. I think this was a sign to find a job near home.

One day Frank walked into the back office. "Anita, have you been checking the warranty e-mails?" he asked.

"No, I haven't," I said.

"Why not?"

"I'm overwhelmed."

"Also, Mary said she gave you an order on Wednesday. Why did you send it to the warehouse on Friday?"

"I'm the only one who's sending orders. I'm overwhelmed," I said.

"Well, that's not good enough!"

"Don't you yell at me! What do you expect? You put a lot of pressure on me, and it's not fair."

He walked away.

What a nitwit. How dare he tell me it wasn't good enough? Oh my God, I had to leave before I cracked his skull or wound up in a place I didn't want to be. I went out for a full hour. I needed air and gather my thoughts. It was a cold December day, and I went to get my diamond necklace cleaned at Kay Jewelers. It was across the street from Macy's. When I approached the saleslady, I began to cry.

"Oh no. What's wrong?" she asked.

I was choked up, and I couldn't speak. I put my hand up to tell her to wait. I controlled myself and said, "My boss is a damn nitwit."

She smiled and said, "I know. I've worked for many bosses like that. I just wanted to punch them in their mouths."

I laughed. "That's for sure. I'm here to get my necklace cleaned."

"Sure. It will take about ten minutes. I'll be back."

"OK."

I walked outside to get some cold air and looked across the street. Macy's had on the front of the building, in glittery big letters, the word "*Believe*." I smiled and cried, and I said to myself, "I do believe. I do." Funny thing was I hadn't seen it when I was walking down the street earlier. The following day I received a call about a position in Brooklyn near my house. I went on the interview and I got the job. You have to *Believe*.

Everyone knew Roll-On's business was not good because there were a lot of people calling for money. Post office threatened to pick up the stamp machine for non payment.

Frank called everyone into the showroom and said, "Please, sit down." We did, and he said, "We are leaving to Las Vegas for the show. We are hoping we get a lot of orders because Roll-On is going through a rough patch. We might have to let people go. We will cut your pay by twenty percent; the health insurance will be cut, and you will have to work longer hours. And you will be happy doing it. I hope everyone is onboard."

Where did he think he was? He was living in his own world. No one was going to stay in a company that kept taking and taking, and they had to like it.

After everyone left, Tom and Frank were still sitting in the show-room room. I walked back into the showroom.

"I'm glad both of you are here," I said. "Frank, do you remember when you said to Vicky that if she didn't like it here, she could leave?"

"Yes, I remember telling her that," he said.

"Well, I'm not happy here and I'm resigning."

"Really, I'm sorry to hear that," said Tom.

"You are one of the few people I hate to see you leave" said Frank.

It felt good and I felt so relieved. The best part is that my last two weeks here Tom and Frank with be in Las Vegas. And I would never see them again.

After I resigned Mary told me that every girl they hired after I left was either fired or never came back. They were on employee number five. That seems to be the number.

Fifteen

SCOTT LEWIS

Scott Lewis was a men's apparel company. They manufactured shirts and ties. They licensed out shoes, socks, and suits. Their office and warehouse were in Brooklyn, in a three-story building that they owned. They also rented out office space to painters, pattern maker, bike company, spa-equipment company, and a milk company, to name a few.

During my phone interview with a man named Matt, he said I would be replacing someone in the office with whom he was not happy with. I really didn't like the area the office was in, but it was a twenty-minute walk from my house.

Matt was a thin man with glasses. He was about five feet tall, and his hair was thinning. He seemed very serious and stiff.

When I first walked into the office, there were employees there. It was an office with two big rooms with desks, five small offices, and a showroom.

We spoke about hours, duties, and salaries.

"So when can you start?" Matt asked.

"In two weeks," I said.

I was hired to enter orders and do customer service. It was hard to start another career when that was what I knew. I wasn't happy with it anymore, but it paid the rent.

There were two owners: Scott and Matt. Scott lived in Israel, and Matt lived in New Jersey.

Matt told me for my first day to come in around nine thirty, so everyone would already be in. When I arrived the receptionist was sitting at her desk, working on a computer.

"Hi. How can I help you?" she asked.

"I'm here to see Matt," I said.

She got up and waved at a Matt, who was sitting in an office with glass walls and a glass door. He waved for me to come over. I walked into his office.

"Hi, Anita," Matt said.

"Hello," I said.

"Please, close the door. Thank you. You are going to be sitting in the empty office for now."

"OK. I have a question. I know you said everyone works from nine to six, but if I come in early—say eight or eight thirty—can I leave at five thirty?"

"Let's keep it like this for now, but nothing is set in stone."

"OK."

Shari was the receptionist; she also did data entry. She'd been with the company for almost two years.

Esther handled the credit and accounts receivables; she had been with the company for six months.

Natasha was the house sales rep. She had been with the company for twenty-five years.

Tally was a designer and had been with the company for eleven years.

Tom handled special orders and was Matt's assistant. He had been with the company for eight months.

Paulette was one of the designers and had been with the company for only two weeks.

Carolyn did the production for the company. She was also new.

Deena did accounts payable and payroll. She had been with the company for a year.

Dan was the warehouse manager, and he had been with the company for eight years.

I met everyone in the office and in the warehouse. There were about fifteen people working there. I knew Matt and Scott would be getting rid of Shari the moment I saw her. They must have worn her down. After finding out how long everyone had been there, I found it troubling but not surprising.

Matt walked over to me and said, "Anita, on Monday you'll be sitting in the front."

"OK." I wasn't too happy about this. It meant I would also be the receptionist. But I need this job, so I put on my big-girl panties and handled it.

On Monday I was the only one in the office. I moved my chair and my supplies to the front desk and got settled. On the wall behind where I would be sitting was a phone and a monitor showing all the security cameras' views. The phone on the wall rang, and I saw Shari outside, waiting to get buzzed in.

I said, "Oh shit, what is she doing here?" I'd thought Matt had told her. Before I buzzed her in, I took my purse and my supplies I'd put in the desk drawers, but I couldn't switch chairs because it was too late. Then I buzzed her in.

I quickly when back to where I had been sitting.

"Good morning," said Shari.

"Good morning," I said.

She sat at her desk and starting working. Then Matt and everyone started walking in.

Around twelve Shari was fired. She took her belongings and left.

Matt came to me and said, "Anita, you can sit at the front now."

"OK." I moved my stuff back and laughed to myself.

—m—

A few days later, Scott walked into the office, looked at me, and said, "Well, hello Anita."

We shook hands, and I said, "Hello, Scott."

"Welcome. We'll talk later."

"OK."

As soon as anyone walked into the office, they saw me. To my left were two small offices where Natasha and Tally sat. To my right was another desk; Tom sat there. On his right was Matt's small office. Next to that was the showroom, with a glass door. In front of Tom were two more small offices. Esther and Carolyn sat there. Then in the second room were Paulette, Alan and Denna and some file cabinets and office supplies.

Scott Lewis would come to the States several times a year for the trade shows and to work on design. He was a very tall man, and he dressed sloppy. His shirt was always out of his pants like he was a bum. A man who owned a men's apparel line selling suits, shirts, and ties should always have been dapper.

On one visit Scott walked into the showroom and pulled a bottle of scotch from his suitcase. He opened it and poured himself a drink.

Carolyn was working with Matt and Scott in the showroom for a while. I saw Matt pouring himself a drink too. Then Carolyn walked into her office, and I could see she was pissed. She was throwing papers around. This went on for a couple of days. At one point Tally was speaking with Carolyn, and it looked like he was trying to console her.

While I was in the bathroom, Carolyn walks in.

"Are you OK?" I asked.

"No. I can't believe they're stressing me. I just can't take it. It's too much work for one person," she said.

"You have to do what's best for you."

"I know and I will."

The next day Carolyn didn't come in, nor did she call to say she would not be coming in. Later that day Tally told us she had sent an e-mail saying she would not be coming back.

Two weeks later one of the freelance designers, Alan, was working with Scott. I heard Alan yelling, "I don't like the way you are talking to me. You have no idea what you're talking about."

I heard a loud noise, and then I saw Alan came out of the showroom. He took his belongings and walked out of the office. He never came back. He had been there for only two months.

That was two people so far. Everyone there was fairly new except for Natasha and Tally. I wondered why. I was sure to find out soon.

—⚊—

One afternoon Matt called me into his office.

"Anita, we need the orders entered from the New York show, but I see lot of open pick tickets," he said.

"I know. There are so many orders, and I haven't had time to invoice yet. It's a lot of work for just me," I said.

I was sitting across from him, and I could smell something awful. I couldn't figure it out until he spoke again. It was his breath. I never saw him eat, and he smoked cigarettes all day. His breath smelled like he had eaten a shit sandwich mixed with cigarettes. I had to cover my nose the whole time he was talking.

"So can you do it?" Matt asked.

"It's a bit overwhelming, but I'll do my best."

———〰———

Esther gave me the scoop about the company. She told me Scott and Matt took advantage of everyone there. Everyone was overwhelmed. She told me that before Carolyn, there had been Amie, who had worked there for two years. When Matt and Scott had felt she was not working enough, they'd decided to cut her pay by 30 percent. She'd resigned after that.

I was working for nitwits again. I must have been a horrible boss in my past life, because this was crazy.

———〰———

One afternoon I was giving Deena some paperwork for my direct deposit.

"Anita, how are you?" she asked.

"I'm OK. And you?" I said.

"I'm OK, but you look overwhelmed."

"Yes, I am, and so do you."

We both laughed.

"I'm leaving the company," she said.

"Really? Why?" I asked.

"It's too much work for one person, and they're not hiring anyone to help me."

"Wow. It seems like everyone is overwhelmed here."

"Yes, and they take advantage of you."

"Yes, I heard," I said.

A few weeks later they hired Jerry to replace Deena. Jerry stayed for only four months and then he resigned. They hired another person, also named Jerry. I hoped he would stay, but it did not look good when the company had a revolving door for employees.

—⚁—

Tally had owned his own tie company in St. Louis. He'd come to New York to work for Scott Lewis. Tally told me that a year earlier, he'd had a heart attack in the office and died for a minute. Scott had not been good to him. He had made Tally sign a waiver stating that if something else happened to him, the company was not responsible. Scott held Tally's bonus until he signed it.

These small companies do whatever they want as long as people allow it. What had I gotten myself into?

Matt and Scott finally hired someone to replace Carolyn in production.

Beare was from Bangladesh, and he had a deep accent. There were times I couldn't understand what he was saying.

It had been six months, and so far everyone was still there.

Scott and Matt purchased another building, and the warehouse was also moving to a larger space. Downstairs, where it was currently, was too small, and there was also merchandise in five other office spaces.

Instead of getting shelves built, running wires for the phones and Internet, and getting the space ready for the merchandise, Scott and Matt just dumped everything into the new warehouse. It was a disaster. Scott had asked for suggestions. I had suggested we close the warehouse for two weeks until everything was straightened out and inventory was counted. Also we should tell the customers we would be shipping in three weeks. That way if we shipped in two weeks, they would be happy. He didn't take my suggestion and told the customers we were shipping in a week. In the end we shipped in four weeks because the warehouse wasn't ready.

Every time Scott visited, he disrupted the office procedures and stressed everyone out. And he used terrible grammar in his e-mails. It was like a kindergartener was writing them. Just because you have money, it doesn't mean you're smart. Common sense is not common.

———❧———

Matt had this belittling way he spoke to Esther and Beare, and I didn't like it one bit. Matt was yelling at Esther about an account. "What is this?"

"Give me a minute, I'm looking for it." said Esther

When he walked out of her office I read his lips and he called Esther a fucking bitch.

I knew he would try to do it to me too. But I would not take crap from anyone there.

One day Matt decided to test me.

"Anita, Marvin Free said you shipped three duplicate tie orders to Paul Michaels. What happened?" he asked.

"I did?"

"Yes, you did. How did you do that? Are you paying attention? The customer is yelling that he received all these ties. Why?" he yelled.

"Don't ever yell at me, you understand? I won't know what happened until I find the paperwork. I will get back to you," I said.

"OK. Let me know. Also did you take care of Carl's order from B Men's Wear?"

"I have been in touch with Carl about his order."

"Really? I find that hard to believe."

My voice went up. "Really? Tell me why you find it hard to believe. Why don't you call Carl and ask him if we spoke about his order?"

"Well, Marvin said that Carl never got it."

"Before you believe what Marvin tells you, ask me first. You always take his side and believe everything he says. I will be right back," I said.

I walked out, slamming the door open, and I said under my breath, "Who the hell does he think he is, yelling at me? I'm not taking his shit or Scott's shit either."

Marvin Free was one of the road salesmen, and we all hated him. He was an ignorant prick and swore he never made mistakes. His initials were perfect for him: MF for motherfucker.

While I was looking for the hard copy of the order for Paul Michaels, I was praying I hadn't made the mistake. I finally found it. Ha—Marvin had written the order twice. Thank God because I never would have heard the end of it.

Matt left for the day, so I would speak with him tomorrow. I was glad because I really didn't want to speak to him now.

As soon as he walked in the next day, he said, "Can I see you in my office?"

I went in, sat down, and covered my nose. I could smell his breath from across the desk, it was so bad. It was like someone was shoveling horse shit in his mouth. It made me nauseous.

"I'm talking to you calmly, with respect," Matt said.

"If you would have done that in the first place, we wouldn't be having this conversation now."

"What happened to the Paul Michaels order?"

"Here it is. Marvin wrote it twice, so it wasn't me. You should call Carl about his order and ask him if we spoke about it."

"You're right, I'm sorry. I should have asked before assuming. Thanks."

"Yeah, you should have. Is that it?" I asked.

"Yes, thank you."

I walked out of his office. What a nitwit.

—❦—

Tom handled the elevator when there were packages and other things for the tenants in the building. Matt always had him running around, making copies of keys or ordering office supplies. Tom was a party guy. He was in his early twenties, and there were times when he would walk into the office drunk like a skunk from the previous night. He had been born in the Midwest and loved Brooklyn.

For a couple of weekends, someone had been having illegal parties in the empty warehouse. One Monday, when I walked into the building, it smelled like beer, and there was graffiti all over the walls. When Scott arrived at the office, he examining the surveillance video. He called Tom into the conference room.

I could hear Tom saying, "Well go ahead. It was not me." Then he walked out of the showroom and sat at his desk.

I looked over at him. "Tom, what's going on?"

"Scott thinks I'm the one having the parties in the building."

"Why would he think that?"

"I came into the building to use the bathroom with two of my girlfriends."

"Why did you come here?"

"I was in the bar down the block."

"Oh."

Scott walked toward Tom. "Come into the showroom. I want to talk to you."

They were in the showroom for about ten minutes. Then Tom walked out, saying, "You will be hearing from my lawyer."

He collected his things and said to everyone, "Hey, guys, I was just fired. He thinks I have something to do with the parties." Then he walked out.

Everyone knew Tom had nothing to do with the parties; he'd even told Matt it was going to happen because he had seen it on Facebook. Matt was pissed that Scott fired Tom. But Scott owned more shares of the business than Matt.

Tom had not been happy there, and I knew he was looking for another job, as we all were.

I was wondering if Scott and Matt were going to hire someone to replace Tom. I had a bad feeling that they would have me do the EDI (electronic data interchange) orders.

—⁓—

Tally called me over to his office.

"What's up?" I asked.

"I'm leaving the company," he said.

"No way. That's fantastic."

"No one knows. I didn't say anything to Natasha yet. Don't say anything."

Natasha and Tally had been friends for eleven years.

"I won't, but when are you telling Scott and Matt?" I asked.

"Next month."

"Wow."

"The best part is that I'm going to the competitor."

"Oh my God, please make sure I am here when you tell them."

We both laughed.

Karma's a bitch, and the owners had not been good to Tally or anyone there. To them it was all about the hours, and they made sure we worked the hours we were supposed to, or they would quickly deduct from our salaries. If anyone owed them hours they had been paid for, Matt was quick to ask when that person would make them up.

A month later Tally resigned and gave his two weeks' notice. He told me that Scott asked him where he was going and why. Tally never told him where but told him why. He said he was not happy about how Scott and Matt had treated him during his heart attack and about holding his bonus. Scott told Tally he couldn't work for a competitor because of the contract he had signed. Scott said he could sue Tally. Tally asked him to show him the contract. Of course there was none. Tally reminded Scott he was very good friends with his wife and spoke to her often. Scott replied that his wife knew about the massages he got. Tally replied that massages weren't the only things he got.

Natasha was now going to design the line with Scott. I was happy for Tally because he was talented, and they didn't deserve him. It was time for me to leave this place also. I seriously had to start looking for another job.

—〰—

Every time Matt called me into his office, it felt like I was being called into the principal's office.

"Please sit," he said.

"What's up?" I asked.

He was smiling, so I knew he needed something.

"I need you to help with the EDI orders until we find someone to replace Tom."

I'd known he was going to dump that on me, but what was I suppose to say, no?

"Sure, as long as it's temporary," I said.

"Yup."

I didn't believe a word Matt said because I had heard him lie to everyone, and I was sure he was lying now.

Over the next few days, he showed me the orders and wished me well. I had to figure out everything on my own because he didn't know either. I was so pissed I had to walk out. I went to my favorite bookstore café Brooklyn Book House. They have the best coffee, pasteries and books.

—〰—

Matt and Scott decided to hire a temp for order entry and invoicing. I was happy because I couldn't do it all myself.

Matt walked over to me and said, "Anita, we have a temp coming in today, so please show her the system."

"Sure," I said.

Layla had a one-year-old son and was looking for permanent work.

I showed Layla the system once, and she caught on quickly. I showed her one time, and she was off on her own. I hoped they kept her because she was good.

After a few weeks, Matt asked me, "Anita, how's Layla doing?"

"She's good," I said.

After four months he offered her the job. Everyone was happy—especially me because I didn't have to do it any longer.

I couldn't believe I'd been there for more than a year already. Since I had started, Scott and Matt had not spoken to or treated people fairly.

There was one time when Beare needed to leave at five thirty, and we usually got out at six. That day I was also leaving at five thirty; I sent Matt and Scott an e-mail that morning to let them know. Matt told Beare he should have sent an e-mail early in the day, like I had. He said no to Beare, who sat back down and continued his work. What was half an hour when there were times when Beare worked on the weekend? He always eats lunch at his desk.

One day Esther was out, but she still worked thirty-eight hours that week. Matt still deducted a day from her pay. He and Scott gave her a hard time, but she fought them and got paid for the day. Matt then told her she had to work forty-five hours a week. She said that by law it was forty hours a week, not forty-five. The owners tried to take advantage when someone was on salary instead of hourly.

If they had told Paulette she couldn't work more than forty hours, then why say the normal rate was forty-five? It didn't make sense. Paulette got paid hourly, and the owners didn't want to pay her over time. It was all about the hours and how much they could take advantage of us.

—⁓—

At every show Natasha worked on trimming the booth, packing, and unpacking, and Scott and Matt never helped her. She was always fighting with them. Scott was always stressing her out. He and Matt drank liquor all day while at shows and in the office too.

Jim was one of the sales reps for New York; he had the major accounts, like Kohl's, J. C. Penney, Macy's, and so on. He had been in sales for more than twenty-five years. He had been with Scott Lewis for ten.

One day Jim came into the office to meet everyone and talk about how he could make things better for everyone. He wanted to manage the office. He handed out a survey about how we feel about the company. Everyone filled it out anonymously. Jim spoke to Matt and Scott about it. Scott was interested in everyones comments, but Matt didn't care.

This was a small company; it did not have a Human Resources person, and Scott and Matt didn't post the days off. Someone always had to ask if the office was closing for a holiday. For one of the Jewish holidays, Matt said on the day before that he would be closing the office, but we would have to work on Saturday or Sunday to make up for it. I worked from home and showed him proof with e-mails and EDI orders.

After I sent an e-mail regarding the hours I had worked from home, Jim and Matt had the nerve to ask me why it had taken me three hours to work on Kohl's routing. I told both of them that I felt insulted, and how would they know to put a time on what I did when they had never done it before? Especially when this was new to me. They never mentioned it again because they knew they were wrong.

I was still a bit confused about the EDI orders because Matt had thrown me to the wolves. It was like reading a foreign book. These orders got loaded into our system, and it was very complicated. All of the major accounts had their own vendor manuals, and they used a lot of tricky words, so we could fail and receive charge-backs. This was how they made their money. They were the mafia of chargebacks.

I had done EDI in the past, and I'd never liked doing it. On one of the Kohl's orders, they had cancelled a purchase order and revised it with a different purchase-order number. Usually they just revised the start and cancel dates with the same purchase-order number. I noticed it happened again but with J. C. Penney.

I called Jim about the three orders. "Hi, Jim."

"Hi, Anita, what's up?"

"I'm calling you about the three orders for J.C. Penney. Can they be the same as the one for Kohl's? I'm confused."

"It's a dummy PO—not an Anita PO."

"Fuck you, Jim. Find someone else to do it."

"You know if I was someone else I would curse you out."

"I wish you would. I promise that I will bring cursing to a new level. Who do you think you're talking to? You know, you are no different from Matt and Scott. You are made from the same fabric." I hung up on him. How dare he?

I knew I would not last long in this company with the way they ran things. No one there was professional.

———※———

Layla needed to change her hours because she needed to pick up her son by six. She sent an e-mail to Matt, Jim, and Scott. Of course all three did not like the way she had written the e-mail. They felt like she was demanding to change her hours. Layla showed me the e-mail, and she had not demanded it. They were a bunch for fucking nitwits. I saw how they tried to take advantage of Layla, but they would find out that she did not take shit either.

———※———

August was busy with the Magic show coming up. There were several trade shows between February and August. Magic was held in Las Vegas in both months. There were also shows in Atlanta, Chicago, and New York. Everyone was going crazy trying to prepare for the last show.

I needed a vacation, so I asked Matt before he walked out the door.

"Matt, I want to request vacation for the end of the month," I said.

"OK. Send me an e-mail."

I sent one to Matt, Scott, and Jim. Ten minutes later I received an e-mail from Matt saying I could not go on vacation because they would be coming back from Magic with many orders, and he hoped I could understand and that they would have my full cooperation.

Jim sent me an e-mail saying it was wrong of Matt to reject my vacation.

I forwarded that to Scott and asked him to call me. The phone rang immediately.

"Hi, Scott," I said when I picked it up. "Did you read my e-mail?"

"Yes, and Matt is right. You cannot go."

"Well, consider this my two weeks' notice." I couldn't believe I'd said it, but I had, and I felt relived.

"OK," Scott said, and we hung up.

I didn't have another job, but I wasn't going to let them stress me out. I would not die of a heart attack in this office.

—⁂—

The phone rang. It was Jim.

"Anita, Scott does not want you to leave the company."

"Then he should tell me"

"You know he never will, but I want to speak to you, Layla, and Esther."

We all went into the showroom and spoke to Jim on speaker phone.

"Hi, ladies," he said. "I would like to talk to you about the orders that will be written at the show. Scott and Matt are saying it should be a couple hundred."

I laughed because I didn't see them writing so many orders.

"Sure, but understand that Anita does not enter orders anymore, so I don't know why they would give her a hard time. She does everything here, and they don't appreciate her," said Layla.

"I totally understand. That's why I'm getting involved," said Jim.

"What happened to the survey we all filled out?" asked Esther.

"Matt said he didn't care," Jim answered.

"I'm not surprised. Now you know what we go through here," I said.

"I can't believe he said that," said Esther.

"I can't believe he said that either," said Jim. "But this is what I spoke to Matt and Scott about: Anita can go on vacation as long as all the orders are entered. We will Federal Express you the orders every day while we're at the show, and that will give you time to enter all of them before we get back."

"OK, but I'm doing it so Anita can go on vacation with her family," Layla said.

"I made a bet with Scott that if all the orders are entered, he will buy me a steak dinner, and I will give you girls manicures and pedicures," Jim said.

"Oh, I like that," said Esther.

I didn't believe a word he said. I would believe it when I saw it.

"Thank you, Layla and Esther, for helping me out," I said, "but I can't believe they have to go through all this shit so I can go on vacation. And I don't even enter orders anymore."

"Anita. I understand your point," said Jim, "but they want you to help out Layla."

"Of course. I will always help her out," I said.

"Anita please don't worry I have this under control" said Layla.

"Thank you" I said.

"Thank you, ladies, and talk to you soon," Jim said.

Natasha, Matt and Scott would be at the show for a week, and I would leave the following week, so I would not see them until after Labor Day.

The show ran from Tuesday to Thursday. They forgot to send the orders to us on Tuesday. We received fifty-six orders on Wednesday and thirty-six on Thursday. So it totaled ninety-two orders. They'd sworn it was going to be a few hundred. All that shit for ninety-two orders. Layla entered all the orders herself. Nitwits.

I went on vacation, and I never went back to Scott Lewis. I sent an e-mail to Matt, Scott and everyone in the office:

> Hi All,
> I will not be coming back to Scott Lewis, and this is why: you are unprofessional, and you speak to your employees very disrespectful and you take advantage of everyone in the office. We all work hard for you, and you don't appreciate it.
>
> Scott, you have no common sense. Your spelling is embarrassing. Matt, your breath smells like shit, and everyone hates you. Your business is failing, and everyone is going to Tally's new business.
>
> I will not have a heart attack because of you stressing me out. Have a good day.
> Anita Martini

Sixteen

Freelance Gigs

Pastel

After a few calls to the agency 24Seven, they called me back and told me that Pastel needed me to freelance for them again, but it was for a different division. The project was for only three months, and it started the next day. I said yes. I would be working in production on the men's wear line (hoodies only).

I liked freelancing for Pastel because their offices were right on Thirty-Fourth Street, and they had ice cream parties. I love working in the city. I would be reporting to a woman named Keyold.

Keyold was in charge of the production of men's hoodies. She'd worked for Pastel for about three years. She was married and had a three-year-old child.

At first I was friendly and tried talking to her, but that was not working. Keyold was very sour with me from day one. I had to sit next to her in a moon-shaped cubicle. I just did my work and didn't say a word to her all day. She left me notes about what to do, and once I was done I replied back with notes. Once in a while she would say she was going out to lunch or leaving for the day. All I would say was, "OK."

One day, while I was busy working on some costing Keyold had given me, someone said, "Hi."

I turned around and said, "Hello."

"I'm looking for Keyold. Do you know where she is?"

"No, sorry, I don't."

"OK. Tell her Marcy came by. We have an appointment."

"OK, I'll let her know."

Ten minutes passed, and Keyold wasn't back. I decided I would leave her a note when I came back from the bathroom.

When I got back to my desk, she was on the phone, chitchatting with someone. Twenty minutes later she hung up.

"Marcy came by to see you," I said.

"Oh, shit. Why didn't you tell me?"

"You were on the phone."

"Shit." She grabbed her notebook and left.

Someone was late. I grinned. She was such a bitch, and I was there to help her.

When she got back from her appointment, Keyold grabbed her bag and said, "Anita, here are some cards and swatches. Can you put them together? I'm going to lunch." I was surprised that she had said anything to me—not that I cared.

I didn't have a chance to answer, as she was already gone. She was rude. I had to remember I was there for only three months. When she got back, I was at my desk, finishing the last card. I lined the cards up and handed them to her.

"All done," I said.

She took them and put them on her desk. She didn't even say thank you.

I grabbed my bag and said, "I'm going to lunch." I didn't give her a chance to answer as I walked away.

Even at freelancing gigs, there were bitches. But why should it have been surprising?

When I got back from lunch, Keyold had left me a note: "Here are more cards to finish. See you in the morning."

Oh great, I will have all afternoon without her. I finished all the cards before going home, and I was glad because when she walked in the next day all the cards would be waiting.

While I was making copies of the cards, one of the girls approached me.

"Hi, how are you?" she said.

"Good and you?" I replied.

"I'm Margaret. You work with Keyold, right?"

"Yes, I'm freelancing. I'm Anita."

"Good for you. I applaud you because she's a bitch and very rude. I can't stand her. She can't keep anyone who freelances for her."

"Really? Wow, that's not good." I finished making my copies. "Thanks for the heads-up."

"You're welcome. See you around."

"Sure. Wait, is she nice to you?" I asked.

"She's not warm," Margaret said. "She's like that, but not to everyone. Too bad—you seem like a nice person."

"Thanks."

After a few weeks, Keyold was still sour with me, but I really didn't care. It was for only three months. I knew it was not me because everyone in the office was nice to me, and it was a huge office with many people.

I was entering some styles one morning when Cynthia came over. She sat a few cubicles away from Keyold.

"Hi, Anita," Cynthia said.

"Hi, Cynthia," I said as I continued entering the styles.

"Ready?" she asked Keyold.

"Yes," Keyold said. She got up, and they left.

I saw everyone else leaving the office. I stayed at my desk; Keyold hadn't invited me, so I continued to work.

"Hey, are you coming?"

I turned around. "Hey, Margaret."

"Come on."

"Where?"

"To the ice cream party upstairs," she said.

"Oh, thanks. OK. I love your ice cream parties."

"I know it's great"

While waiting on line, I heard, "Anita." I turned around. It was Celeste.

"Hi, Anita, how are you?"

"Hi, Celeste. I'm good, and yourself?"

She kissed me hello, and from the corner of my eye I saw Keyold watching.

"Good, thanks. Are you freelancing with us again?" Celeste asked.

"Yes."

"Who are you working with?"

"Keyold," I said.

"Ouch. She is so very rude."

"I know."

"I don't like her. Not many people do."

The next morning I was in the kitchen, making coffee and putting my lunch in the refrigerator, when Margaret approached me.

"Hi, Anita," she said.

"Hello, Margaret," I said.

"You know, between you and me, Keyold complained about you to the big boss."

"Really? Why?"

"Because she's a bitch, and the best part is that the big boss got back to her and said, 'You know, I find it hard to believe because everyone liked her in the other division.'"

"Really? Wow, thanks for telling me."

"I thought you should know."

"Thanks."

Karma's a bitch.

When I walked into the kitchen to get my lunch, Margaret was there, and so was Keyold.

"So we meet again," Margaret said.

I smiled at her. "Yes, we meet again."

Keyold walked away. Margaret and I gave each other looks that said, *She's got an attitude.*

"Oh, shit!" I couldn't find my lunch in the fridge. I started looking through everything. "Damn!"

"What happened?" Margaret asked.

"I think someone ate my lunch. It's not in here," I said.

"What?"

"My lunch is missing."

"You know, that happens here."

I stood up and said, "Who the hell eats some else's lunch? I would never. That is disgusting."

"What was it?"

"Pizza."

"Sorry."

"It's OK. I hope they enjoyed it."

I walked over to my desk and wrote a note for whoever took my lunch. It said: "I hope you enjoyed my lunch." I went and put it up on the refrigerator.

Later on that day, I went back to check if anyone had removed the note. Someone had written back: "Thanks. It was great!"

I snatched the note and wrote: "I hope you enjoyed the special sauce."

Later the person replied: "I did."

I ripped up the note, and that was the last time I brought in my lunch and kept it in the fridge.

—⟲—

K eyold was at her desk, but I didn't say anything to her. I sat down and started my work. Cynthia came by.

"Ready?" she asked Keyold. "Hi, Anita."

"Yes, let's go," Keyold said.

"Hi, Cynthia," I said.

Keyold said, "Be back later."

"OK."

I finished the cards she had given me and placed them on her desk. Her mouse moved and her monitor turned on. There was an e-mail to Cynthia on it, and at the bottom was a complaint about me. It said: "I'm so tired. I want to go home. I'm not really happy with my temp."

I looked around and hit "print." Then I turned her computer off. Women are bitches. That was why no one liked Keyold.

When I got home, the agency called me and said that was my last day at Pastel. A few days later, the agency called me to freelance at the Bloomingdale's corporate offices.

Bloomingdale's

The offices were on Third Avenue and Fifty-Sixth Street. I'd never liked working in that area because it was hard to find somewhere to get food. I would have to walk a few blocks to get pizza or a burger; but it was a job, and I would have to deal with it. Lunch was the least of my worries.

The company occupied the tenth, eleventh, and twelfth floors. I had to go to the reception area on the tenth floor. As soon as I walked in, I knew the receptionist was stank: her face was stuck on attitude. She had a hairdo I called "the combo." On one side of her head were finger waves; there were some curls on the top; and on the other side she had a ponytail. It was more like a combo of disaster.

The job was for only a month, and it was for the Bloomingdale's online business. I would be sitting in a big conference room with other temps doing the same job: checking the website for typos and adding colors. I would be working on the furniture section. The other temps had clothing, shoes, and so on—anything Bloomingdale's sold on its website.

There were five of us temping together. In the conference room, there were several long, black tables facing the walls, each with a computer and a chair. During a break we would all turn our chairs around and chat for a minute, or one of the girls would show us something she saw online about a celebrity.

As we walked through the offices, it felt like I was in the scene from *Working Girl* when Melanie Griffin walked to her desk, and all you saw was a row of women at their desks. It was like a planet of only women. Sigh. You know when you work with women, all their cycles sync up, and they all get their periods at the same time. Can you imagine about a hundred women all PMSing at the same time? Bitch City.

We would all go to lunch together, and I loved walking past all those pretentious bitches. Some would smile, some would scrunch up their noses, and some wouldn't even look at us. I could tell they were young and worked late hours just to be in fashion. I was done with it—been there, done that. It was like walking the hall of shame, but just because we were temps, that didn't mean we were losers. I'd rather be working as a temp than be a slave to my job. I had done that for many years. I had paid my debt. I felt free and not stressed at all. And I didn't have to wonder if I was gonna get fired.

In the beginning of the fourth week, the company extended my job for one more month. I was happy because their sample sale was starting the next week, and of course I had not found a full-time job. The other temps were also extended for a month.

Paula was one of the temps. She was nice and looked a lot like Mariah Carey. She worked across from me with three other girls: Carmen, Daisy, and Macie.

Whenever anyone pissed off Paula, she would change her seat. One day the rest of us came back from lunch, and she had moved all of her stuff to another computer. I found it so funny. I'd never seen that happen, but I'd heard of someone who'd done that before. I looked at her, and she winked at me. We both smiled. I liked her. None of the other girls said a word to her.

Carmen was a hot mess. She was the temp queen. She worked during the summer in New York and then in the winter flew out to the Caribbean, where her family lived. What a life, huh? She was obsessed with celebrities. During lunch she would spend her time online, to see what the celebrities were wearing. She loved Angelina Jolie and followed what she was up to.

Daisy was four feet nothing with enormous boobs, and they were real. They were always out there, and she was not afraid to show them. She was a mother of five and was looking for a boyfriend. She wanted to get married. During lunch she would always yell at her kids over the phone.

Macie was all over the place, and so were her outfits. One day she wanted to be a designer, and the next day she wanted to sign up for the army. Every day was a surprise. She loved fashion. I remembered when I'd loved fashion, but it was not the same anymore.

If you ever want to get into the fashion industry, you'd better come correct. You'd better be talented and know your stuff; otherwise people will take advantage of you.

—m—

One afternoon when all the other temps and I got back from lunch, there was a pizza party going on in the first conference room. It was the first room you saw when you walked into the office. Everyone was there. When we all looked toward the conference room, the receptionist and several girls looked our way. We all turned around and kept walking like it was the end of a runway.

We all looked at each other, and I said, "Well, we are temps." We all laughed.

Paula said, "Thank God."

Carmen said, "Aye, I can't wait to leave New York."

Daisy turned to Paula and asked, "Is my blouse dirty?"

I smiled to myself because Daisy was the type to always soil her tops. It was because her boobs were way too big. She needed a bib.

As we all sat down to work, the receptionist walked in.

"Excuse me, ladies," she said, and then she giggled. She was nervous. We all stared at her. "Would anyone like some pizza?"

Paula said, "No thank you. We've already eaten."

No one else said a word.

"OK. Thank you," the receptionist said and then walked away fast.

We all raised our eyebrows, pressed our lips together, and then turned around and continued working.

Two weeks later the receptionist walked in. "Good morning, ladies," she said.

We all turned around, looked at each other, and then said good morning to her too.

"Ladies, we are having a pizza party today, and we would love for you to join us," she said.

There was silence, and then I said, "Sure." Then everyone repeated my answer.

After the receptionist walked away, we all looked at each other.

Paula said, "Why did she invite us? Was she feeling guilty from the last time?"

I said, "Yeah, that was a guilty lunch invitation."

Paula said, "She invited us because there was extra pizza last time, and no one wanted it."

We all laughed.

Macie said, "I'm ready for a free lunch."

Daisy said, "Uh, I want some free lunch too."

I looked at Paula, and we both opened our eyes wide. *Damn!*

When the month was over, the other temps and I went our separate ways. I had a few months before I started another freelance gig, but it was only for the month of December. After that I would figure it out.

Vestiti Dolce

The job was only for the month of December, and the uniform was black only. It worked for me because I loved wearing black. It was clean and classic. And I loved New York City in the winter, especially in December.

Although I would be working for one of the most famous Italian designers, I was not a bit excited. It was only good on paper, and that wasn't worth anything. The company's offices were located in SoHo, and I got there fast from Brooklyn. I missed working in SoHo. I loved it there too.

I looked through my closet and drawers, pulling out everything black, which was most of the clothes I had. On my first day, I wore a fitted black turtleneck with an A-line, black leather skirt; a three quarter button-down, soft, buttery leather jacket; and black leather boots.

The company's offices were not as extravagant as I'd thought they would be; they were more loft-like. I walked into the reception area.

"Hi, I'm here to see David Mills," I told the receptionist.

"Sure," she said, "and your name is?"

"Anita Martini."

"Please have a seat, and I'll let him know you're here."

I saw a man walking toward me. "Anita," he said.

"Yes."

We shook hands.

"Hi, I'm David Mills. Come, let's walk to the back."

David Mills had been with the company for ten years. He was very pleasant and professional.

It was market week, and I was assigned to help with the models, straighten up the showroom, and do order entry. It was great because I was in at 9:00 a.m. and out by 6:00 p.m. at forty dollars an hour. I was good.

David walked me to the offices and intruded. "Come, Anita, let me introduce you to Katia. You will be assisting her with orders."

"OK," I said.

"The kitchen is right over there, and you can help yourself to coffee or whatever you want. It's fully stocked."

"Thank you."

They had an awesome espresso machine. It could brew a cappuccino like no other. I drank one every morning. They supplied lunch too, and they weren't cheap lunches either.

Everyone seemed nice, but as soon as I saw Katia, I knew she had attitude. I spotted her as soon as I walked in.

"Katia, this is Anita," David said. "She will be assisting you with the orders."

"Hi, Anita."

"Hi, Katia."

Katia worked for the sales department. As soon as I saw her, I knew she was pretentious and uptight. I would bet the farm she flaunted where she worked. I did it too, and I got anything I wanted. Everyone wanted to be your friend so they could get a discount and never pay retail. After working in wholesale for years, it was very hard to pay retail for anything.

The first week was crazy, but on Friday things slowed down a bit. I was helping Katia enter orders. It was ten to six. I went to the bathroom before going home. I got back to my desk, and I saw Katia coming my way, smiling. She never smiled at me. She had to want something from me.

"Hi, Anita," she said.

Oh boy. She wanted me to do something for her. "Yes?" I said.

"Can you stay a little late to help me with the orders?"

I smiled back and said, "Sorry, I can't. I have to leave at six o'clock."

She stopped smiling and said, "Oh. OK. Thanks."

It felt so good to say no because there was nothing she could do about it. I was only freelancing, and I was really enjoying it.

After a month I was getting tired of wearing only black; I needed color. The month had gone by fast, and I was off to find a full-time job.

Seventeen

Edward Jones

While freelancing at Vestiti Dolce, I was always looking through *Women's Wear Daily* for a job. I'm getting tired of this business, I need a change. Then I came across an ad for an operations manager in Long Island, for a luxury hat and handbag company.

At first I didn't know if I wanted to leave the city, but I needed a job. It had been eight months. And for some strange reason, I knew I was going to get the job. Finally I decided to e-mail my resume, and someone e-mailed immediately about an interview. That should have been a sign.

When I came out of the train station, the area was isolated: there were car dealerships and industrial companies, and that was it. On the next block was a big building with several floors. That was where I was going.

When I got to the third floor, there was a glass window, behind which two girls sat. They buzzed me in. As I approached the front office, a Spanish girl with long, black hair opened the door. She had on jeans with a tight-fitting top and stilettos. I knew from looking at her that she would be a problem. I saw right through her.

"Hi, I'm here to see Sammi Franco," I said.

She smiled and said, "Sure. Your name?"

"Anita Martini."

"You can sit here. I'll let her know you're here."

"OK."

While I sat and waited for Sammi, I checked out the girls in the office and the vibe. I could tell the morale was very low.

A blond woman walked over to me, extended her hand, and said, "Hi, I'm Sammi Franco."

"Hi, I'm Anita Martini."

"Let me get you an application to fill out. I'll be right back."

"OK."

While I waited I saw the spanish girl laughing on the phone and swinging her hair around. The other girl was working.

Sammi returned. "Can you please fill out this application? I'll be right back."

"OK."

Once I was done, I handed Sammi the paperwork. She said, "Come, let's walk over to another office. This one belongs to the warehouse manager."

It was a big office/small inventory room. There were many boxes with hats and trims. We spoke about the position, salary and the duties. They needed someone to start right away because the person in the position was leaving on Friday, and it was already Tuesday.

Sammi Franco was a consultant. She had been with the company for only a few months, but she'd been in the business for more twenty years. I liked her right away. She was more on the IT side but knew all the aspects of running a fashion company. She knew her shit and was good at her job. Everyone called her Sammi F. because there were two Sammi's in the office.

After we spoke about the job, she introduced me to the warehouse manager, Andy.

Andy had been with Edward Jones for fifteen years. He was from the Middle East and always wore house sandals in the warehouse, which was an OSHA violation. The regulation stated that steel-toed boots were to be worn in any warehouse, but Andy did whatever he wanted.

After Andy was paged several times, he walked into the office. He looked at me and then at Sammi and said, "What?"

Sammi looked at me, and I looked at her. I knew it was not going to be good. The man was a prick.

"Andy, this is Anita. I'm interviewing her for the operations position," Sammi said.

He smirked and said, "Well, this is a factory where we have to be every day and not screw up the orders. They have to be entered correctly."

Just as I had thought. The whole time that he was talking about the factory rules, he didn't look at me once. I was sure he was going to be a problem. While he went on and on about how the orders had to be right, I thought, *I hope I don't have to report to this prick because I will not take the job.* Then it got better: Edward Jones walked into the room.

Edward Jones was the designer and the owner. He was a very pale man who'd had either too many chemical peels or too much Botox because his face was so shiny and tight. He had shoulder-length, blond hair; it looked greasy and dirty. He did not have a clue about how to use a computer. Edward was a strange character, and he appeared to be difficult to work with.

Only time would tell if I would be able to work with Edward, but my first impressions had not been wrong in the past. Sammi introduced us. Edward sat down and looked at me.

"So, if something is late, what should you do?" he asked.

"It depends on several things. I would have to check the order, see what account it is, check the cancel date, see when and if the goods are coming in, and talk to sales to see what's going on."

"Very good, and thank you," said Edward. Then he walked away.

"OK, Anita. Let me speak with Edward, and I will get back to you," said Sammi.

"OK. Thanks."

That was quick. When I walked out, I was not comfortable with the area. I was sure it would be better in the summer because at 6:00 p.m., it was still daylight out, but in the winter it got dark earlier. I still needed a job, though.

Sammi called me on Wednesday and asked if I could start the next day. I agreed. I was even able to squeeze in a few more thousand dollars after three months.

"Welcome aboard," she said.

"Thanks. Oh, by the way, who will I be reporting to?" I asked.

"Edward."

"OK, good. I would have to decline if I had to report to Andy. I will not be taking any of his shit."

She laughed and said, "I don't take his shit either."

"Good, so we're on the same page. See you tomorrow."

"See you tomorrow."

I got the job, but to be honest I really wasn't feeling the location. But the pay was good.

—m—

On my first day, I was dressed for war in a black shirt and camouflage pants. To be honest I didn't care. I would be working in a dirty warehouse anyway. Sammi took me around to meet everyone in the warehouse. The majority of the workers were Hispanic, and I was able to communicate with them. They were hardworking people. There were fifteen workers in the warehouse and five people, including me, in the front office. I would be supervising the two girls up front and the shipping area of the warehouse. Lucy and Deborah both sat in front of the glass window so they could buzz people in.

Lucy was the receptionist. She had been with the company for two years. She answers the phone and entered orders. Lucy was a young, Spanish single mom. She always looked like she had worked the pole the night before. Tight jeans, low-cut tops, and stilettos were inappropriate for an office even if it was in a warehouse.

Deborah had been with the company for two years. She handled orders, invoices, and everything else Lucy shoved her way. Deborah was married and had older children. She was from the Middle East. She was wonderful and worked hard at her job.

Sammi Jenatkis had been with Edward Jones for eight years. He knew how things worked there. He was the graphic designer and in charge of the website and photography. Everyone called him Sammi J. because he and the consultant had the same first name.

I worked with Sony for the next two days. He ran all the reports and showed me everything he did. I asked a lot of questions, especially about the company.

Sony had been at Edward Jones for only three months and was already leaving. He'd found a job near his home. He'd been traveling all the way from New Jersey. He really didn't say much, only that he was happy he was leaving. He also said I would be the fifth person in the position in two years.

Wow, you got to be kidding me. Oh my God, there I went again. Déjà vu. I started to feel dizzy. Why did I always find myself in that type of companies? Sigh. I wanted to throw myself on the floor and cry. I had to put on my big-girl panties and handle it. I had to do what I had to do. I would see how long I would last. Damn! I took a deep breath and moved on.

Friday was Sony's last day, and he was pissed. He told me Edward owed him for four days and was not going to pay him for them. I had been there for only two days. That was not a good indication of how people were treated in the company. Damn, man! This was bullshit. Sigh. I guessed it was better to see it upfront rather than later. I think this is my last stop.

As the orders came in, it started to get very busy. Fall was one of the busiest shipping seasons. Time went by fast, and then we went home.

Every time I would walk into the office, Lucy would be on Facebook, chatting with friends. As soon as she saw me opening the door through the small mirror she had glued on her computer screen, she would switch to the order-entry screen like she was working. I let it go, but if it continued I would have to speak to her. I knew it would happen again.

Lucy walked over to my desk one day, smiling. "Hey, Anita, do you want to have lunch?" she asked.

"Sure," I said. She knew I had seen her switching her screen. That was why she was being nice. I saw right through her.

Lucy drove to work every day, so we took her car. I took the train every day. She lived somewhere in Queens. As we walked toward her car, I saw her throwing her hair in the wind and flaunting her fake boobs. She did that when she saw a man. I said to myself, *Oh boy. She's a tramp, and she is looking for attention.*

Lucy chatted about work and her ex's not giving her enough child-support money for her three kids. She did all the talking; I just listened.

"You know, before you there were four other supervisors. One of them was always trying to get me to go out with him. I kept saying no, and then finally I said yes. We went out like three or four times, but then I called it off."

"Why? What happened?" I asked.

"He was harassing me, so I filed a sexual harassment suit."

"Oh, wow. So what happened?" Why was she telling me all this?

"Nothing. They fired him, and that was it," Lucy said.

"Oh, I see."

She was trying to get friendly with me so I would let her do whatever she wanted, but that was not going to happen.

When we went up to the office, she said, "Oh, I want to show you something. You know Candace from the New York office?"

"Yeah. Why?"

"Do you know what she looks like?"

"No," I said.

"Can I show you, it's on facebook? I'm going to log in ok?"

"Go ahead."

She logged onto Facebook and went to Candace's page.

Candace worked as an admin in the New York showroom. She had been with the company for six years. The times I spoke to her, she seemed like a nice girl. She did her work and I liked her.

Lucy showed me pictures of Candace in lingerie and pointed out where all of her piercings and tattoos were. As she continued to talk, I realized that all of my thoughts about Lucy were true. She was not a good person. She thought it was cool to be on a social media site while working, and it was not. Why would she do that to Candace? All I did was smile and listen. I didn't trust her.

I would alternate with both Deborah and Lucy because someone always had to cover the front desk. I would rather have lunch with Deborah because she was a mature woman, and she was real.

The next day Deborah and I had lunch. There was a cafeteria one flight down; it was cheap, and the food was good. Of course I grilled her. I asked her many questions about the company. I was hoping I was not right about what I thought.

Deborah spilled her guts. She said Edward was crazy. During photo shoots he'd light incense and play music for good karma. He would let Andy yell at everyone in the warehouse, even curse at them. She said Lucy was a bitch, and she did what she wanted because the company was afraid she might sue them.

I was always in before or by 9:00 a.m., and Deborah was always there before me because she started at 8:30 a.m.

When I walked in, she said, "Good morning."

"Good morning, Deborah," I said.

"How's it going?"

"It's good. By the way I need to see that order Lucy was having trouble with."

"Sure. Here it is," Deborah said.

"Thanks."

I was working with Deborah at Lucy's desk when Lucy walked in at nine fifteen with her fake Gucci shades on. She didn't look happy about my being in the office before her or that I was sitting at her desk.

As soon as she walked in, she said, "Good morning."

"Good morning," Deborah and I both said in reply. I got up from her desk and went to mine. She threw her purse in her drawer and looked at Deborah as if to say, *Damn, I'm late.*

I didn't say anything to her, but I would start noting the time she got in. I walked back to my desk and started my day. Later I walked over to Lucy and handed her a pile of orders she'd entered the day before.

"Oh, by the way, here are the orders you entered yesterday. The lines that are highlighted are the ones that are missing," I said.

Every time Lucy entered a large order, there were mistakes. When I found them, she would be upset. If she would enter them correctly, she wouldn't have to get upset.

"Oh, OK. I'll fix them right away," Lucy said.

"OK, thank you."

When I walked away, she moved over to Deborah and whispered, "Can you help me with these orders?"

I overheard her, and I walked over. "Deborah, did you finish those invoices I gave you?"

"Yes, I did, but I just got a lot more from the warehouse to do."

"OK. Thanks. Come with me. I want to show you something."

She walked over to my desk.

"Listen," I said, "I don't want you helping Lucy because she does not have a lot on her plate, and she can do it herself."

"Yes, I know. She's always throwing her work on me," Deborah said.

"Yes, I know that. I've seen her do it, but it will stop. When she approaches you, tell her you have too much to do. She's too busy on Facebook."

"Oh, you know about that?" Deborah asked.

"Yes, I do."

"Damn, you are good."

"I pay attention."

I walked over to the warehouse to check on shipping. When I came back to the front office, Lucy was chatting on Facebook once again. I stopped and looked through the window and waited for a while. But as soon as I walked in, she switched it off quickly to a fake excel sheet. She didn't even know how to use Excel.

I walked to my desk, and Lucy came over. "Oh, here are the orders I fixed. Can you check to see if they're correct?" she asked.

"Sure," I said.

The orders were finally correct. I gave them back to her.

"You want to do lunch?" she asked.

"No, I can't today. I have some errands I have to run."

"Oh. OK."

When I got back from running errands, I saw that Deborah was taking pictures with her phone of Lucy in sexy positions. I had a serious look on my face when I entered the office.

"Hello, ladies," I said.

Lucy was in shock that I had caught her. Deborah gave me a worried look. I gave Lucy a look and thought, *Hello, you know that was not appropriate in the office.* I did not say anything, but I wrote down the incident. She would either shape up or ship out. Her behavior was not OK. I knew she'd put Deborah in awkward situations.

The next morning I walked in, and I could smell incense. Edward was shooting his new spring line for the website and catalogue. He had it burning all day. Lucy was in on time because she knew there was a photo shoot that day, and Edward would be in the front office.

—⟋⟋—

Sammi F. came in only three days a week: Monday, Wednesday, and Friday. As soon as she walked in one morning, I went over to her.

"Good morning," I said.

"Good morning, Anita. How's it going?" she asked.

"Good, but I need to speak to you about an issue."

"Sure."

"Let's walk to the back," I said.

As we walked to the back, Andy was watching us. He never said good morning to me, so I didn't say it either. If I said good morning to a person and that person didn't reply, that would be the last time I did so. Andy always thought that Sammi F. and I were up to something when we walked around the warehouse.

"What's up?" Sammi F. asked.

"I want you to remove Lucy's option to go on Facebook or any other non-work-related sites."

"I have seen her on Facebook. When I come into the office, she switches it off," Sammi F. said.

"Yeah, she's done that to me too. Why is the company allowing her to do it? Plus she does nothing. If she has any orders, she tries to push them off on Deborah," I said.

"I was planning on removing the option from her computer, but Edward has me doing all this nonsense work for him. I will take care of it now."

"Perfect. Thanks."

The next day Lucy walked in with her shades, and she though she looked good.

"Good morning," she said.

Deborah and I said good morning.

Lucy opened her drawer, threw her bag in, and took off her shades. She turned her computer on, and I walked to the warehouse.

When I walked back to the office, Lucy asked, "Are we having a problem with the server?"

I said, "I don't think so. Why?"

"Were you able to get in the EDI program?"

"Yes," I said.

"OK. Thanks."

Deborah and I looked at each other, and we smiled because we both knew why she was asking. She must have tried to get on Facebook and couldn't. I didn't like her, and I would fire her very soon.

—◊—

Lucy and Deborah walked over to me. Lucy said, "Anita, we were supposed to get reviews last year. Right, Deborah? Do you think it will happen this year?"

I looked at Deborah because I was sure Lucy had told her to come and talk to me.

Deborah said, "Yes, she is right."

"OK. Let me talk to Edward and see what he says," I told them.

That afternoon I spoke to Edward. He asked me to write up the reviews. I went to accounting right away for the paperwork so those girls could finally get raises.

There were four people in the accounting office.

Isaac had been with Edward Jones since he'd opened his business. He was the head of Accounting and Human Resources. He was an older man; probably he should have been retired.

John would do the taxes for the company and other things. He was retired but came in part time. He had been with the company for eight years.

May was also older but not at retirement age. She handled imports and customs. She had been with the company for twelve years.

Douglass handled all website orders, returns, and credit cards. He had been with the company for ten years.

Isaac was very helpful and never rude. John was listening to my conversation with Isaac about the reviews. May and Douglass were busy on the phone.

"Good luck," John said

"Thanks I'm going to need it," I said

I knew what he meant and he knew what I meant.

I walked back into the office and said, "Ladies, I spoke to Edward, and I have the paperwork here for your reviews. I will fill it out and then speak with each of you."

They both said, "OK."

I went over the paperwork with Deborah and Lucy separately. They both signed the papers, and then I gave them to Edward.

A week later Lucy walked over to my desk. "So, any word on my raise?" she asked.

"No, not yet. Edward hasn't said anything to me."

"You want to go to lunch?"

I really didn't want to go, but it would be the last time I would go out with her. "Sure, but I can't stay long. Let's go downstairs to the deli."

"I don't like going there," Lucy said.

"Why?"

She didn't answer, and we went downstairs anyway. When we got to the deli, Sarah was beind the counter and her father Havi was cooking on the grill. Sarah and her father Havi had been here for ten years.

"Hey, Anita, how are you?"

"I'm good, Sarah, and you?" I replied.

"We have gyros today." said Havi

"Hey Havi how are you, yes give me one."

I noticed Lucy and Sarah were cold toward each other.

While we were waiting for our lunch, Lucy opened up again. "You know Sammi J., the graphic designer?"

"Yeah, I like him. He's nice," I said.

"I'm having an affair with him, and he's married." She seemed so proud of it.

"Really?"

"Yeah, he calls me at home all the time, and my sons love him."

"Oh." That was all I said. I was wondering why she was telling me this. All I did was listen.

Lucy got her sandwich first. "I'm going to grab a table," she said.

"OK."

When Sarah handed me my gyro, she said, "I can't stand that bitch. She walks around like her shit doesn't stink. One day she tried yelling at my father about her lunch."

"Really? What did your father say?" I asked.

"'Don't come here again if you don't like it.'"

"Good for him. Thanks for telling me, and thanks for the gyro. They are so good."

"Have a good lunch, Anita."

"Thanks Sarah."

———ɷ———

Before Sony, Frida had been the supervisor, and she had been very friendly with Lucy. They would take two-hour lunches and dump all the work on poor Deborah. They'd never invited her to lunch. Lucy and Frida had even joined a gym together. Sammi F. told me Frida never did her job and was always on personal calls with her sister in Jamaica. After five months she was fired.

Before Frida it had been the supervisor Lucy had the affair with. She then filed a sexual harassment suit against him and Edward Jones. Now I knew why she got away with things.

In the fifteen years that the company had been in business, I was supervisor number thirteen. So there was almost a person a year in the position, and I could see why.

Both Deborah and Lucy approached my desk.

"What's up, ladies?" I asked.

Lucy pushed Deborah ahead of her so she could speak first. Lucy was very sneaky.

"Yes, Lucy?" I asked.

She giggled. "Any word on our reviews?"

"I gave them to Edward. He said he'll going to get back to me. I will ask him again."

Lucy moved Deborah over. "Well, we haven't gotten a raise in two years. Edward keeps saying soon, soon, soon, and then nothing. Then we wind up with a new supervisor, and we have to wait again."

"I will speak to him and then get back to you."

"OK. Thanks."

Deborah said, "Thanks, Anita."

Everyone went back to work. Several days later I saw Edward.

"Good morning, Anita." He was all smiles, probably because his hair was washed.

"Good morning. I want to talk to you about Deborah and Lucy's reviews and raises."

"You know money is tight. They might not get anything this year," Edward said.

"So you're telling me no?" I asked.

"Right, I'm telling you no."

"OK, I will let them know."

Edward smiled and said, "OK." Then he walked away, waddling like a duck.

After lunch I called Deborah and Lucy over. "Please sit. I spoke to Edward, and he said money is tight, so there will be no raises this year."

Lucy said, "OK, but I need more money, so I'm going to speak to him myself."

"I'm just telling you what he told me. You do what you have to do," I said.

Lucy had an attitude all day, but that was beyond my control. If she wanted to talk to Edward, I couldn't stop her.

I was in the bathroom, washing my hands, when Deborah walked in.

"Listen, I'm going to try to get you guys more money, but you know how this company works. Edward is stingy," I said.

"Yeah, I know, but it's been almost two years and nothing. Plus every time we talk to a new supervisor about our raises, they get fired," Deborah said.

"Yes, I know, and I will be next."

"Why do you say that?"

"Because I know. Believe me, I know."

The bathroom door opened. It was Lucy. As soon as she saw Deborah and me talking, she walked right out like a child. Deborah was going after her when I grabbed her arm.

"Let her go. She'll get over it," I said.

We both laughed.

"It seems like you know her very well," Deborah said.

"Yeah, I know her type. You know she's going to ask you what we were talking about."

"Yeah, I know," Deborah said.

"Tell her the truth. It's not like we were talking about her."

When I returned to the office after working out some issues in the warehouse, I heard Deborah and Lucy talking. They did not see me or hear me come in.

"Deborah, can I borrow twenty dollars?" Lucy asked.

"I don't have it," Deborah said.

"Are you sure?"

"I told you I don't have any money."

"Well, I don't believe you. Let me check your purse." Lucy went to open Deborah's drawer.

"Don't you dare. If I tell you I don't have money, it's because I don't," Deborah said.

Lucy smirked and kept on entering orders. She took advantage of Deborah. She had borrowed money from Deborah before and never paid her back. It was Deborah's fault for allowing it. What a bitch Lucy was. I couldn't wait to fire her.

"Hi, ladies," I said.

They both said hi.

Lucy got up and said, "I'm going to lunch." She grabbed her purse and went toward the warehouse.

"We'll talk when she leaves," Deborah said without turning her chair around.

I said, "OK."

We saw Lucy take the elevator. As soon as the doors closed, I rolled my chair over to Deborah.

"What's going on?" I asked.

"She's trying to force money out of me," Deborah said.

"I'm glad you told her no because she likes to take advantage of you, and it's not right."

"Can you believe last week she asked me to watch her children for the weekend?"

"No way! And what did you say?" I asked.

"I told her no. I'm not a fool."

"Good. She's not getting a raise because her performance is poor, but I will try to get you one," I said.

"When Frida was here, Lucy bragged to me that she had gotten a raise."

"Did you get one?"

"No!"

"Wait a minute. Lucy got a raise; you didn't; and then she bragged about it?"

"Yes."

"Don't worry this will not happen with me around—trust me."

"I know, and thank God for you. Between the sexual harassment lawsuit and then Lucy's being friendly with Frida, I can't take it anymore."

We both laughed.

"Everyone has their day," I said.

"They sure do. Thank you."

—ᴍ—

Besides shipping to the major department stores, we had a website where we sold retail. One morning I received calls from four customers who had received the wrong merchandise. I searched for all the orders and invoices to see what they had ordered and what had been shipped. I noticed that the orders had Andy's signature on them, so that meant he'd picked, packed, and shipped the orders. I walked over to him with all the paperwork, and I saw from his face that he already had an attitude.

"Hey, Andy, I have four customers who called me because they received the wrong merchandise," I said.

He immediately put his glasses on and tried to snatch the papers from my hands, but I didn't let go. He looked at me, and I said, "Don't snatch the papers from my hands. I can hand them to you, plus I didn't finish what I was saying."

Andy gave me a dirty look, and I looked at him too. He spoke to the people in the warehouse with such disrespect that I just wanted to punch him in his face.

"OK. Leave these papers with me. I want to check them," he said.

"Sure," I said and then walked away.

When I got back to my desk, Sammi F. was waiting for me with a smile.

"What's up?" I asked.

"I received several e-mails from customers who received the wrong merchandise, and Andy packed the orders."

"How do you know it was him?" I asked.

"I have the paperwork," said Sammi F.

"I just spoke to him about that," I said. "He was just beefing with me about four orders I gave him that he also shipped wrong."

"This is additional from what you have."

We both laughed. Andy thought we were troublemakers because we would call him out on things, and he hated it. He'd had problems with all the operations managers because he was supposed to report directly to them. That made me his boss.

"So are you going to give him the news?" I asked.

"Sure. Care to join me?" Sammi F. asked with a smile.

"Sure, let's go."

"I'm sure we're going to add to his madness when he finds out he shipped out more orders incorrectly."

As we walked toward the warehouse, we heard Andy yelling. "You stupid idiot. What the fuck are you doing?"

He was yelling at one of the workers. When we arrived he walked to his office and looked at us.

"Why are you coming over here for? To bullshit about my mistake?" he asked.

I smiled and looked at Sammi F. She quickly said, "Hey, that's not nice. Watch your mouth."

"You both came over here looking to blame me."

Sammi F. said, "Listen, Andy, I came here to speak to you and to find out what happened because I have four more orders that were shipped wrong." She handed him the invoices. "These are the orders the customers e-mailed me. I stapled the e-mails on top, so you can see what they said they got and what was supposed to be shipped."

"So why are you coming to me? Did I ship them?" Andy asked.

Sammi F. took an invoice and looked through it for the initials. We already knew they were his. "Is this your signature?" she asked.

He pressed his lips together. "Yeah, I think. Leave them here, and I'll ship them today. And why did you both have to come here and blame me?"

I stepped in. "We're just asking you about the mistakes, not blaming you."

Sammi F. said, "I just asked you a question. We all make errors."

"Yeah, yeah, OK. I will ship them. I'm sorry. Good-bye."

Sammi and I looked at each other. We were in shock that Andy had apologized.

As we walked back to the office, I said to Sammi, "He said sorry, right?"

"Can you believe that?" she asked.

"No."

We both laughed.

"Does Edward know how he yells at them back here?" I asked.

"Yes, he does. He feels it will keep them in line. He's never said it, but I know that's it."

"I'm sure you're right." My heart dropped because it wasn't right. But I couldn't fight for the warehouse employees because they allowed Andy to abuse them. That would not happen to me. Ever!

How could Edward know better when he had never ever worked for anyone? He was a trust-fund baby who was somewhat artistic, with an uncle who owned a major convention center in the garment industry. Part of me thought he had to know better, and he was just playing ignorant.

Some of the workers talked to me about how bad Edward was and about all of the people who had worked for the company in the past. They also talked about how horrible Andy was to them. They even said to watch out for Lucy; she was a snake.

Natalie was Andy's pet. She could do no wrong. She had worked for the company for twelve years, as the shipping manager. She'd gotten pregnant by one of the workers.

Edward wanted Natalie to train someone to cover her while she was on maternity leave. Edward and Sammi F. were doing the interviewing for her replacement. They hired someone, and Natalie trained him. Then Edward asked me to do the returns, which meant opening boxes and logging returns for repairs. At first I was not happy about the new assignment, but then I enjoyed it because I was in the warehouse, and no one bothered me. I also learned about the merchandise.

When Natalie came back from maternity leave, Edward did not place her back as the shipping manager. She was doing returns, and she was not happy. I heard Edward say he didn't want to give her back the position because she had a newborn and would be out a lot. That was not good.

The new shipping manager, Javier, had been with the company for only six months when he decided to leave for another job that paid more money. He spoke to Edward and Sammi F., and they presented him with a counteroffer. Javier stayed. A month later he was fired.

It was a really fucked-up place. Someone told me that was not the first time Edward had presented an employee with a counteroffer, the employee took the bait, and then he fired the employee a month later. Wow.

After he fired Javier, Natalie asked Edward for her job back, and he said no. He promoted someone else and told her to train him for her position. She was livid, but she had to do it to keep her job. I even asked Edward to bring her back, and he told me no. So that was it—I couldn't help her.

The last straw came when Edward and Sammi F. asked me to speak to Natalie about training me. I knew she would say no because I would have said no. Edward had taken advantage of her. He couldn't forget that he came from a woman, too…I think.

"Natalie, can I talk to you?" I asked.

"Sure. I want to tell you to be careful with Lucy. She's a snake," Natalie said.

"Yeah, I know. Listen, Edward wants you to train me on what you do."

"No," she said.

"No?"

"No."

"OK, I totally understand." I walked away.

Edward and Sammi F. were in the office, so it was a perfect time to tell them. "Regarding Natalie training me, she said no," I told them.

Edward said, "What?"

"I said, she said no. She is not going to train me."

"Really? OK. Sammi F., come with me," Edward said.

"OK," she said.

They walked away, and fifteen minutes later I saw Natalie walking out. They had fired her. She had taken the bait.

The next day I saw Sammi F. I walked out before she opened the door to the office.

"Listen, we have to get rid of Lucy. She takes advantage of Deborah. Plus Deborah can do the job alone. Lucy is upset because she needs more money, and honestly she's not getting it. I'd rather fire her and give a nice raise to Deborah. Andy is another problem. My goal is to fire both Lucy and Andy."

"I agree, but Andy has been here for fifteen years. It's going to be hard to fire him," Sammi F. said.

"It's not impossible. Edward did it many years ago. Andy came crawling back for his job, and Edward took him back."

"How do you know that?" Sammi F. asked.

"People talk, and I listen," I said.

"Edward is coming this way. Let's talk to him."

"Hi," Edward said.

"Can we talk to you in private?" Sammi F. asked.

"Sure," he said.

No one had ever entered Edward's main office. I could only imagine what was in there that he didn't want anyone to see. I would have loved to sneak in to see what he had in there. He was such a weirdo. We spoke in his little office, where there was a table, a few chairs, and some light fixtures.

I said, "I want to talk to you about Lucy."

"What about her?" he asked.

"She has been using the Internet to chat with friends during company hours, and I asked Sammi F. to restrict her from going on certain sites. Lucy wants a raise, and she was going to ask you after I told her you said there is no money for raises this year. I think we should let her go and give her responsibilities to Deborah. She can do it all by herself, and you can save money by giving Deborah a nice raise. Lucy also has bad energy. And what about Andy? Can we fire him too?" I was on a roll.

Edward asked me, "Are you going to take Andy's place?"

"No, but we can hire someone."

"We'll see. Talk with you guys later," Edward said and then walked away.

Sammi F. looked at me. "I can't believe you said all that."

"Well, it's the truth. Plus Andy's a piece of shit. Between the tramp and that shit working here, things are not going to change."

"I know."

—∞—

I noticed that every morning when I went to my desk, it looked different. The orders were not like I'd left them. So I decided to booby-trap it. I had some orders that Andy wanted to see, but I didn't want to give them to him yet. I placed a note with the orders underneath a pile of papers.

The note said, "Andy, do not touch my orders, and mind your own business."

The next morning I walked in and searched my desk. I couldn't believe that he had written on the note I'd left, "I won't touch the orders."

He had fallen for it, and I'd proved he was looking through my desk. That son of a bitch.

When Lucy came back from lunch, she walked over to me and asked with an attitude, "Well, did you talk to Edward about my raise?"

"Yes. I just spoke to him, and he said there is no money."

"OK."

She went back to work. Before she went home, I noticed she was cleaning her desk and throwing out lots of paper. She left at 5:30 p.m., and I left at six.

After Lucy left I searched her garbage. She had thrown out all the orders that were going to ship and a lot of other papers.

The next morning, when I was walking to the warehouse, I saw Sammi F. and Edward walking toward the office.

"Good morning," they said.

"Good morning. Can I talk to you guys for a minute?" I asked.

We went to the little office, and I closed the door.

"Listen, last night Lucy threw out all the orders and paperwork on her desk," I said.

"What? Why did she do that?" Edward asked.

"She needs to be fired."

"She's right. We do need to fire her," said Sammi F.

"OK. Thanks. Anita, let me speak with Sammi F.," said Edward.

"OK."

When I returned to my desk, Lucy came over.

"I know why I'm not getting a raise. Because you didn't fight for me. You're nothing but a lowlife," she said.

She must have been out of her mind. "What?"

She walked away, and I said, "Don't you walk away from me. I'm talking to you." I followed her out of the office. I caught up to her in the hallway.

"Let me tell you something," I said. "I spoke to Edward about you and Deborah. I told him you haven't gotten a raise in almost two years. How dare you talk to me like that?"

"I'm going to ask him myself," Lucy said.

"Then you do that," I said.

She put her hands on her hips, swung her hair around, and went all Spanish *novela* on me. *"El no te quiere,"* she said—"he doesn't want you." *"Tu esta en competencia."* "You are competing against me."

I was so confused. "Who? Wait a minute. You just said I'm competing against you?"

"You said you like Sammi J. He doesn't want you," Lucy said.

I laughed so hard that my mascara was running. "You gotta be kidding me. I like him like I like Sammi F., Deborah, and everyone else, you idiot. I am appalled that you would even call me a lowlife. And another thing—your work performance is very low, and you need to step it up. You're always on your cell phone and on Facebook. That's why you are not getting a raise."

"I'm not on Facebook anymore."

"Yeah, because you're restricted from using it," I said.

I went back to my desk. Lucy went to demand a meeting with Edward and Sammi F.

A short while later, Sammi F. came out and said to me, "Anita, can you come, please?"

We went into the office; Lucy and Edward were waiting for us.

Lucy said, "I need more money. Why are you not giving me a raise? You can pay me with one of your invoices. Why can't you give me more money? You spend money on other stupid things, and I deserve it."

"How dare you talk to me like that? I said you are not getting a raise, and that is final," Edward said.

Lucy stomped out of the office.

Edward said, "Anita, get the key card from her."

I went toward the stairs. "Lucy, where are you going? I need to talk to you."

"I can't. I have to go." She kept on going down.

I walked back into the office, and I said to Edward and Sammi F., "She left."

"Sammi, shut her computer down and delete her access. I will cancel her key card. Remember to change all the passwords. Anita, tomorrow morning when she comes in, tell her just to wait for me and Sammi F. so we can speak to her," Edward said.

The following morning Lucy was at the office door. Her key card was not working. I told Deborah to buzz her in. Lucy sat at her desk and started her day.

"My computer isn't working. I can't log on," she said.

"Sammi F. and Edward want to speak with you," I said.

"About what? And why is my computer not letting me log on?"

"I'm not at liberty to say anything. You have to wait for them."

While she waited Lucy started walking around the warehouse, telling her woes to everyone, but they all knew she was a bitch. She went around telling everyone I was jealous of her. Please. There wasn't an inch of her that I was jealous of. She had fake breasts and a flat ass, and she had been arrested for leaving her young children at home alone when a fire broke out next door. Plus she dated married men. And I was supposed to be jealous of her?

Deborah and I were waiting for Sammi F. and Edward to get in. I called Sammi on her cell phone. She was parking her car and would be on her way up soon.

"Good morning," I said to her when she came in.

"Good morning, ladies. Where is she?"

I said, "In the warehouse."

"Why did you let her go there?" Sammi F. asked.

"I'm not getting involved. I may just hit her," I said.

Edward walked in, and so did Lucy. We all went into the small office.

Lucy asked, "Why does Sammi F. have to be here? She's not my boss."

Edward said, "I want her here."

"Well, I don't."

"It's not about what you want. I'm the owner, and I say she stays."

"I need more money, and you won't give it to me. And Anita, you know what you did," Lucy said.

"Really? What did I do? Say it. Tell them," I said.

She stayed quiet because she had nothing. But I noticed she was leaning sideways and lifting the side of her purse. She had a tape recorder. It was so obvious, but no one else noticed.

"Anita tell her," said Edward

"You are being relieved of your duties," I said

"Why? I came to work," Lucy said.

"If you were ready to work today, then why did you throw out all the orders and your notes and paperwork?" Sammi F said.

She turned pale and said, "You know what you did."

"Then say it!" I said.

"Is that it?" She got up and walked out.

Edward walked her out to make sure she left the office. Then he went into his office, and Sammi F. and I went back to the front office.

"So what happened?" Deborah asked.

I said, "That's it. She is gone."

"What a relief," said Deborah.

"It sure is," said Sammi F.

"You know she was recording us," I said.

"Really? How do you know?" Deborah asked.

"The way she was sitting with her purse. It was held up so she could record us talking."

"She cannot do anything about it. I'm glad she's gone," Sammi F said.

"Me too, and you will get a raise and take over her responsibilities," I said.

"Thank you," Deborah said.

Andy was next.

The front office was great, and Deborah was happy. She had been doing all the work anyway. Now with her getting a little more money, we knew the work would be done, and I was there to help her. The air was cleaner, and it was nice to come to work.

One afternoon I was coming up from the cafeteria after getting a burger, and I saw Andy in the office, peeling an orange and throwing the rind on the floor.

I said, "What is that? Why are you throwing that on the floor?"

He didn't answer me. He walked away. I followed him to the warehouse. "Hello, I'm talking to you. Why did you do that?"

He smirked and said, "Don't worry. She'll pick it up."

"Who?"

"Deborah," he said.

"Well, you need to pick it up and do that in your office." I walked away. He was a nitwit.

When I got back to the office, Deborah had already picked up the orange peels.

"What was that all about?" I asked.

"Oh, back in our country, men peel oranges, and the women pick them up," she said.

"Really? Well he's in the United States, and that will not happen again. Please don't ever pick them up again."

"He was not going to pick them up," Deborah said.

"And you shouldn't either," I said.

We both laughed.

Andy continued to make mistakes on the web shipments, and I had to tell him about them. It was bad enough he hated all of the operations managers, and I knew why he hated me: he couldn't boss me around, and he knew that, and so did everyone else.

His mistakes started to decrease sales and increase returns, which Edward was questioning. He wanted to have a meeting with Andy, Sammi F., and me. He wanted to know why there were so many mistakes on the shipments. Christmas was coming, and he wanted to find out what the problem was.

Edward said, "Anita, can you tell me why there are so many mistakes on our web orders?"

"Well…" I looked at Andy. "There have been many returns due to the wrong styles being sent out."

"Who's packing the web orders?" Edward asked.

Andy yelled, "It was me, OK?"

Edward turned red. "What is going on with you, Andy? I think you're getting too old. I want all the Christmas orders shipped correctly."

"I'm fine, and I do a good job. Ever since she got here, now everyone is looking at me. Let her ship them, then."

I looked at Sammi F., and she shook her head in disappointment.

I was not going to let him talk to me like that. "Why are you blaming me? I didn't pack those orders, and I didn't tell Edward about them," I said.

Edward said, "It was Isaac who told me because he looks at the report every day. It's his job to inform me."

Andy said, "I'm sorry. I will be careful," and then he walked away.

Sammi F. and I looked at each other.

"Wow, I can't believe he apologized again," she said.

"Yeah, because he knows he fucked up," I said.

When Isaac gave me my next paycheck, he said to me, "Here's your check, and I'm sorry to say you are not getting a Christmas bonus. I can't believe you're the only one Edward did not give a bonus to."

"Really? Thanks for telling me. I'm used to working for people like Edward. I know where I stand here."

Wow, I really didn't need to know that. I worked hard everywhere I went, and I still had to work for nitwits. Nothing had changed.

———❦———

During the yearly inventory, things were not adding up. There were many units missing, and Andy had no clue what had happened to them. He was probably selling the merchandise out of a truck.

We kept getting more calls from customers who had received the wrong merchandise. What sealed the deal was the shipment to Saks. Andy had shipped it too early. Isaac told Edward Saks had received a $5,000 charge-back for early shipment. Edward was pissed.

Sammi F. and Edward had several meetings together. I knew they were interviewing for Andy's position. I was glad he was being fired because he was verbally abusive and rude to the workers. Edward was the same way: rude to his employees.

As soon as I saw the person they were interviewing, I went to Sammi F. "Interviewing?" I asked.

"Yeah. Andy will be out of here real soon," she said.

We high-fived.

"It's been a long time coming. I know Edward wants to replace Andy, but to be honest the man you are interviewing is worse than Andy."

"How do you know that?" Sammi F. asked.

"He seems arrogant, and he thinks he knows everything."

"Really? How can you tell?"

"I just know. You'll see."

Andy was fired that Friday, and Edward and Sammi hired the man I'd told them not to. But what did I know?

Stu Shapiro had been in the shipping business for more than thirty-five years, or so he said. That was what he bragged. I didn't like him from the day he was interviewed. He was introduced to everyone, and then he started to learn our system and what everyone did at the company. Sammi F. worked with him on several company procedures. He was a bit aggressive with her. Stu was kind of rude. He tried to tell Sammi F. how to do her job.

The workers were happy that Andy was—hopefully—gone for good because he'd called them stupid and fired them for breathing the wrong way.

After Stu was with the company for a month, I saw him going back and forth. There seemed to be a problem. Hmm, something was going on.

The phone rang, and it snapped me out of my daze. It was a freight company telling me we had requested them to come back. I asked why and who had requested it. He said Stu Shapiro, and they were in the loading dock downstairs waiting. I said OK and that I would tell him.

I knew something was wrong. I immediately called the New York showroom.

"Hey, Candace, how are you?" I said.

"I'm good, you? Are you happy Lucy is gone?" she asked.

"We all are happy here."

"You know she called me and said you got street on her?"

"I sure did, and she's lucky I didn't kick her ass. Another thing I want to tell you. Do you know she went on your Facebook page and showed me all your pictures in lingerie and where all your tattoos are?"

"Wow, she did that?" Candace asked.

"Yeah, and if I were you, I would cut all ties with her."

"Believe me, I will."

"Can I speak to John?" I asked.

"Sure, hold on."

"Hey, I-need-a Martini," John said when he picked up the phone.

"Yes, I need one, too—badly. Listen, do you know anything about this shipment coming back?"

"Yes, it's for La Rouge. Stu said he was calling back the shipment because he needed to add a hat."

"OK. Thanks."

John had been with the company for ten years. He was the sales manager for the New York area.

La Rouge was a European account that had ordered a specific style of hat. We had to ship the entire order. Stu had forgotten the hat.

I hung up from the call with John and then walked out to the warehouse. I saw Stu going back to his office. I walked in behind him.

"Hey, Stu, what's going on with the shipment to La Rouge?" I asked.

"Nothing. I can handle it," he said.

"Why is it coming back?"

"It's not your concern. Don't worry about it."

"What do you mean it's not my concern? You get the merchandise ready and packed; I get it to its destination."

"Well, you're not in that pay rate for me to tell you," Stu said.

I looked to my left and then to my right. I got really close to Stu and said, "Who the hell do you think you're talking to?"

He didn't say a word. He was shocked. I walked away because I was about to lose my damn mind.

It was not going to work. One of us would be leaving, and I was sure it would be me. Stu was worse than Andy—believe it.

Sammi F. and Deborah were talking in the office when I walked in. They saw how pissed I was.

"What's going on?" Sammi asked.

"Stu called a shipment back and doesn't want to tell me why. But I know it was because he didn't ship it complete. He had to call it back because he forgot the special hat that was ordered. It was stated on the order that it must ship complete. I asked him why he was calling the order back, and he said it was not within my pay rate for him to tell me. Then I lost it."

Deborah said, "Oh my Lord, he is a jerk."

Sammi F asked, "Do you know what he did to me?"

"No. What?"

"First of all he's very rude, and I can't stand him. When he came in here, he banged on the desk, asking for a report. I told him I don't work for him and that he's disrespectful. And that was not the first time he'd banged on my desk. He's like a caveman."

We all laughed so hard. Then I stopped when Stu opened the door. Stu walked into the office and asked me, "Do you have a minute?"

"What?"

"I'm really sorry about not telling you," he said.

"You didn't want to tell me because you thought I would tell Edward about what you did, and you were sadly mistaken. We're a team, and if you screw up, we all screw up. Why worry Edward about these small problems?"

Stu extended his hand, but I didn't shake it. I walked back to my office. I knew my days were numbered there.

Several days later Lucy appeared in the office. Deborah and I were the only ones in the front office. She turned to me and said, "Anita, I just buzzed Lucy in."

"Why is she here?" I asked.

"She's picking up her check."

"OK. Call accounting to see if they have it."

I was ready to give that tramp the beat down she deserved plus all of my years of frustration, but I was afraid of what I would do. While Deborah was talking to accounting, Lucy approached me at my desk. I stood up and she put her finger near my face and said, "Yeah, you me fired, but you're nothing but a fucking lowlife."

"You'd better get your finger out of my face," I said.

"Or what, bitch?" She shoved me and then spat in my face.

That is all I remember.

Eighteen

I'm up to Here

I tried opening my eyes, but sunlight was coming in through the window. I tried moving. My arms were restrained. When I finally focused and looked down, I saw I was sitting in a wheelchair, in a straightjacket, overlooking a river, but I wasn't sure where I was. I was really sleepy and very confused. As I sat there for a while, trying to focus, I saw on the other side of the river there was an old sign that said, "East River Bank." Finally I realized I was in Bellevue Hospital.

I heard footsteps coming toward me. I turned around to see who it was. A lady in a cop uniform bent down to talk to me. I moved back and She said, "Ni?"

Only my family and friends called me Ni.

"China?" At first I thought I was dreaming and then I asked her, "What are you doing here?"

China was her nickname; her real name was Miriam. We had gone to high school together. We'd always kept in touch. She was one of my best friends. She was also a cop.

She laughed, then she got serious. "What the hell happened?"

"Why am I here?" I asked.

"You don't remember, do you?"

"All I remember is that bitch spitting in my face and shoving me. What did I do?"

"It's on YouTube."

"How did it get there?"

"You sent it."

"I did? Where is it?" I asked.

She showed me on my phone. "It went viral. You got more than five million hits."

As the video was playing, I opened my mouth wide. Then I laughed hysterically. I looked at China, and she put her hand over her mouth, trying not to laugh out loud.

I got real serious and said, "That bitch deserved it. She's lucky I didn't crack her skull. That's assault! She paid for all the people I've worked for who thought it was OK to bully their employees or coworkers."

I didn't realize it, but after Lucy had spat in my face I had gone ballistic. I had punched her in her face and knocked her out cold. Then I'd locked the front office door. No one was able to come in or out. But everyone in the warehouse was looking through the windows and the door to see what was going on.

I'd set up my phone and taped it. I picked Lucy up from the floor and sat her down on a chair in the middle of the office. Then I taped her mouth and taped her arms and legs to the chair. Meanwhile she was still knocked out. I heard myself saying on the video, "Bitch, are you out of your fucking mind, spitting in my face? You know you can get killed like that. You'd better start respecting people. Who do you think you are?"

Then I started opening drawers, looking for something. There was a pair of scissors.

"Bingo." I walked over to Lucy and looked at the phone. "This is how you take care of bullies." I started cutting her hair. It was almost to her waist, and she didn't like anyone touching it.

I heard a bang on the video. Someone yelled, "Anita, open the door! Open the door!" I looked up. It was Edward. I gave him the middle finger and then said, "Fuck you. If you weren't such a fucking asshole, I wouldn't have to go there. You created this shit."

"I'm going to call the cops," he said.

"Go ahead."

Everyone's mouths dropped as they watched me. Lucy was now awake. She couldn't move, and all she did was cry.

"You see what happens when you push people?" I said to Lucy.

I didn't stop until all of her hair was gone. I left her with bald spots. I uploaded the video and then I pushed the chair away from me, took my phone, and moved to the door to surrender to the cops. When I opened the door, all the workers cheered.

"No need to handcuff me. I will go willingly," I said. I was taken out in handcuffs anyway—with a smile on my face. I walked out with my head held high.

A few months later, I got a call from the *Wall Street Journal*, asking questions about Natalie and the gender-bias lawsuit she had filed against Edward Jones. I told the reporter I had no clue about a lawsuit, but what Edward had done to her was wrong. They settled out of court and fired Stu for sexually harassment.

I think I'm done with the fashion industry.

Made in the USA
Middletown, DE
23 May 2015